saints alive

saints alive

by
James R. Adair

introduction
by
Dr. A. W. Tozer

"Sing unto the Lord,
    O ye saints of His, and give thanks
at the remembrance of His holiness." PSALM 30:4

Biography Index Reprint Series

 BOOKS FOR LIBRARIES PRESS
FREEPORT, NEW YORK

STANDARD BOOK NUMBER:

8369-8011-5

LIBRARY OF CONGRESS CATALOG CARD NUMBER:

76-117319

PRINTED IN THE UNITED STATES OF AMERICA

to a saint

Some call her Susie,
others call her Sue,
I call her Mom.
Like she says,

" 'Hitherto hath the Lord helped us.' "

Contents

Introduction

THE AVERAGE CHRISTIAN, should someone call him a saint, is likely to wince a bit and offer some kind of lame demurrer. He cannot quite see himself as a saint.

The reason for this shying away from the term *saint* is that the word has gathered to itself in popular usage a number of meanings which are not too complimentary.

For instance, some persons think of a saint as a hard self-righteous religionist who sets himself up as a judge of other men's matters while accepting without question the fact of his own superior moral eminence. He is always right, but also he is always a bore and always unpopular, and no one wants to be like him.

Others hold a saint to be a pure and holy soul who has reached a place so remote from the ways of mankind that the simple homely things of the world have no attraction for him. He spends his time in prayer and holy contemplation, being little more than a disembodied wraith faintly redolent of incense and sweet perfume. He is saintly, to be sure, but too much so for comfort. It is easy to understand why persons with this idea of sainthood say, "I am no saint." It is much the same as saying, "I'm no angel," and though it may be a nice, humble way to feel, still it is not good, for it is based upon error.

Then, to many other persons a saint is a black-clad and angular being sitting in haloed austerity, whose hungry countenance and hollow cheeks would excite pity did not his own unsympathetic stare kill all human feeling before it rises. And another unpleasant thing about this saint is that he is always dead, usually a long while dead, but surely and truly dead or he could not be a saint. Between the "unco guid" saint mentioned before and this saint who is "unco" dead there is not much to choose, so the average person simply dismisses the whole thing with a wry shrug.

There is an old proverb which says "He lies well who comes from a far country," and that, I suppose, means that you can get away with any kind of wild tale if you lay the scene far enough from home and there's no one around to check on you. Many honest persons believe that the stories of the doings of holy men who lived far away and long ago have succeeded in getting themselves believed for the very reason that they did come from a far country and cannot be disproved by the facts.

Others equally honest shake their heads and say: "It is very well to tell us of good men who lived long ago. It may be that in other and more favorable ages some people found it possible to walk with God. But it is so no more. Beside the Sea of Galilee in quieter and more primitive times, with the Lord Himself present to help them, a few men and women may have managed to live good lives. But not any more. Those times are gone for good." There we see unbelief in one of its commonest forms. It will believe in things that are far enough away and long enough agone, but it simply cannot muster sufficient optimism to believe in anything close at hand. The godliness it believes in must be no less than several hundred years old and no nearer than Asia Minor.

The author of this book quietly sets himself to show that there is such a thing as contemporary godliness and that a true saint does not need the protective covering of the centuries to prove himself one. He shows that the real saint is one who has turned to God from idols to serve the true and living God and to wait for His Son from heaven. Sober habiliments do not make a saint, nor self-torture, nor poverty, nor isolation from society. Not any of these, nor all of these, can turn a sinner into a saint; much less can a saint be created by ecclesiastical decree. It is faith that does it, real faith that puts a man through the fires of repentance and brings him broken and defenseless to the shelter of Christ's redeeming blood. Then God receives him and sets him aside as one of his special friends, elect and precious, a son indeed and a saint in the final sense of the word.

When Paul wrote his letters to "all the saints in Christ Jesus" he wrote to plain people such as you and I; not to the rare souls such as Bernard and Francis and Mme. Guyon only, but to the rank and file of believing men and women of every degree of education and every level of society who have left their sins to follow Christ and who find something to do for Him and for mankind as they pass the time of their sojourning here.

Far from being stories of persons who lived long ago and far away, these are stories of present-day men and women whose lives can be inquired into. Except for two who have finished the course of their earthly life, they are available for inspection and interview and any of them will be happy to sit down any time and tell the blessed story of their transformation. And though they come from different countries and from different races, they all have the same message to proclaim. It may take any of several forms in the telling, but the sum of each testimony will be: I have found the Messiah and my heart is satisfied.

Chicago, Ill.   A. W. Tozer

...*he pushed the glass aside*...

1

He's Boss of WHR

B<small>OB</small> L<small>AZEAR</small>, <small>MANAGER</small> of the Wyoming Hereford Ranch, one of the five largest and most famous in the United States situated just outside old Cheyenne, is regarded among cattle breeders as a wise, practical man. But a few wondered if he were "missing some of his marbles" at the 1945 National Western Stock Show at Denver.

Excitement ran feverishly high at the climaxing auction. The blue bloods of the range were on sale and cattlemen were writing checks in five figures. A Hereford bull brought $50,000, a record price. The crowd went wild. Several Hereford breeders elbowed Bob Lazear to the side and urged him to put up his prize bull, Helmsman III, for auction. The guarantee was no less than $100,000.

Lazear refused.

An old breeder, who would rather see white-faced cattle sell at princely prices than eat the beef they would make, spat on the ground and allowed that the man was crazy.

But Lazear had his reason. At the head end of Main Street in the WHR village is a stone monument to old Prince Domino, a one-time famous sire on WHR, whose calves sold for more than a cool million. So, a potential Prince Domino, Helmsman III continued grazing peacefully at the Wyoming Hereford Ranch, blissfully unaware of the $100,000 price tag around his neck.

The bull never made Lazear a million dollars, as did Prince Domino, for he died before he was five years of age. But Helmsman's sons and daughters sold at auction for more than $250,000, to say nothing of WHR "private treaty" sales and the actual descendants that still remain in the WHR breeding herd.

Practical to have kept Helmsman III? Bob Lazear thinks so.

The boss of WHR marked himself as practical when a schoolboy in Chicago. Reared in a Christian home and trained in the Scriptures from early childhood, Lazear received Jesus Christ as his personal Saviour at the age of 12. This, he will tell you, is the most practical thing he has ever done. For this transaction, which took place in his heart in the Sixth Presbyterian Church of Chicago where his father was Sunday-school superintendent, opened the way for the Holy Spirit to purge him of sin and to impart to him the very life of God Himself. That is why Bob Lazear can say today, "It would be inaccurate to say I *try* to 'live' my faith, in being a witness for Him, because I realize there is nothing in me that helps to bring about such a situation, but it is only as the Spirit moves."

The lean and lank WHR boss, who looks typically western in his ten-gallon hat, and with wind-bronzed face, had no idea that he would take to the saddle for his career. At 31 he was a civil engineer, having studied engineering at the University of Michigan. But along came Henry P. Crowell, founder of Quaker Oats, who had just acquired the ranch from a friend who had gone broke running it. Crowell, a staunch Christian and long-time friend of the Lazear family, laid plans for devoting WHR solely to improving beef cattle and picked Bob to manage the property.

The fact that Lazear was an engineer and not a cattleman did not worry Crowell. The main thing was his outstanding testimony for Christ and his ability to think clearly. So, like a lot of other ranchers, Bob learned the business from the bottom up.

Now in his thirty-first year on the ranch, Lazear has built such a reputation for WHR and himself that his judgment of good Herefords is rarely questioned. He will not allow inferior animals in the herd, disposing of any whose marking is off, or whose head is not shaped right. It is not unusual for breeders to telephone long-distance and say: "Bob, I need a couple or three heifers. Pick 'em out, will you?" A few months later the breeders get their heifers sight-unseen. And prices may go as high as $800. A California and eastern Oregon big cattle operator has never set foot on WHR, yet every year buys a carload of bulls (30 to 35 head). His herd totals close to 300 WHR bulls and he says he'll continue to buy them sight-unseen as long as his calves continue to get better year after year.

Wyoming Hereford Ranch, aside from being an important place on maps of cattlemen, is on the itinerary of thousands of sight-seers. Some say it rivals Yellowstone as a tourist attraction. Maybe; maybe not. But Main Street in WHR village is usually as busy as the main drag of the average western cow town on Saturday. The village has a population of exactly 99 residents, including the Lazears and cowhands and their families. They are housed in rows of neat dwellings, one a dormitory bunkhouse for bachelors.

Beyond the country-like village are gleaming fences and barns that get a coat of paint every five years to keep them in tip-top shape. One barn, 75 years old, is as sound as a hickory nut. There's a barn for every purpose, each with running water, electricity, and a heating system.

WHR even has its own fire truck. Always ready for duty at a moment's notice, it has brought under control many a prairie fire that could have blackened thousands of acres of precious grass. Too, the ranch has its telephone system and a unique shopping district. Window-shoppers may ride along the streets and gaze at the finest Herefords money can buy—and a few that money can't buy.

Someday, when building costs return to normal, a little church, with a slender spire, will complete the WHR village. Lazear, always alert to opportunities to present the gospel, wants a place to which he may invite evangelists to hold services. Mention of the proposed church appeared in an article published in *The Saturday Evening Post,* and Lazear promptly got an offer of hardwood for the pulpit from a man in North Carolina. He wrote that he wanted it to be a reminder of the rancher's faith in Christ.

All the ranch hands at WHR—35 to 40 are required to run the place—know of Bob Lazear's stand for the Lord. They cannot help it, for it comes out in just everyday conversation. For instance, in the spring of 1951, during a particularly dry period when the professional rain makers were "cloud seeding" the area, Bob came out about 6:30 one morning to find that a light snow had fallen. "Isn't this wonderful?" he remarked to Ernie Green, WHR's top cowhand who has been around some 30 years.

"Yep, the rain makers must be at work," Ernie observed.

"I know a Rain maker 'upstairs' who beats these fellows down here all to pieces." Ernie and two cowhands with him noticeably assented.

Now and then Bob Lazear will take an employee under wing for spiritual counsel. One former ranch hand, just a lad at that time, with whom he had numerous talks, is now a full-time missionary to the Indians in Arizona. A New York boy spent three summers working at WHR, and had

16

many talks with the boss. Graduated recently from Cornell University, he is now studying in a theological seminary.

At cattle shows, where poker games often become the favorite pastime of cattlemen, Lazear finds other things to do. The men respect him for his firm stand, though they occasionally rib him. Once at a banquet at the exclusive Saddle and Sirloin Club in Chicago, practical jokers squirted a shot of liquor into Bob's iced tea. He took a sip, then pushed the glass aside and continued his meal in dry silence.

So far as WHR goes, Lazear has never laid down any definite rules tabooing non-Christian activities, but everyone knows that liquor is absolutely not tolerated. Cowhands know that cursing gets thumbs down, too. Years before his death, owner Crowell himself laid down the law on that. Each animal is a pet, he pointed out. So he asked that ranch hands refrain from swearing and yelling at the cattle. Lazear admits that the men perhaps sometimes forget and do use profanity when he is not around. "But when they see me coming they quickly remember," he chuckles. "Usually they have red faces when I overhear them take the Lord's name in vain and they turn to face me."

The Lord is also honored in the business office of Wyoming Hereford Ranch: the ranch contributes annually big sums to aid the cause of Christ in many sections of the world. This is in accordance with Crowell's wishes, set forth in a trust, of which the ranch is a unit.

Much of this money comes from the annual October auctions at the fabulous ranch. The show equals many of the expositions in color, big money and excitement. Big white hats from nearly every state and several foreign countries come to bid for the cream of the WHR crop.

At a recent auction big money competition broke out. A sober-faced heifer known as Lady Lill was offered. She looked scarcely old enough to wean, but the breeders wanted her. Bidding reached $19,000. Someone lifted an eyebrow to $19,600. Then John E. Owens, of Riverside, California, raised it $400 and took Lady Lill away for $20,000—the record price for a female of any breed of cattle.

Another calf went for $18,000. Sixty head sold well above an average of $3,000 apiece; which "proved" WHR cattle.

WHR, like any ranch, has its headaches. Lazear has had to call on brother Ed, a Cheyenne lawyer, for aid in prosecuting rustlers. Back in 1921 rustlers actually came into WHR pastures and stole some of the best two-year-old heifers. "It took months to run down this case," Bob recalls. "We finally came across a country schoolteacher who helped us get the information we needed."

The teacher was driving home one week end past an abandoned group of farm buildings. Some men were cropping the ears of the cows and dehorning them. (The WHR cattle brand is tatooed in the ear.) When the teacher came up, the men jumped on their horses and rode away, and all that was left were a few cattle with bleeding heads and a pile of horns at the end of a chute.

The culprit, who was later rounded up, had overlooked one tatoo and Attorney Ed Lazear based his case on that animal. The thief was duly jailed. "Mr. Crowell was concerned about the man's family," Bob Lazear recalled, "but we think they got along better without him than beforehand."

The WHR Hereford herd totals 40 bulls and about 850 cows. The hundreds of calves born each year come close to being worth their weight in gold, but they are not pampered. They have to stand the rigors of Wyoming weather, for hardiness is one of the things for which Bob Lazear breeds.

When WHR's Bob Lazear is not talking cattle, he might be taking or showing color pictures (his only real hobby) of his three sons—Bob, Jr., a Presbyterian missionary in Colombia, South America; Jerry, in the cattle feed business in Missouri, and George, ex-Navy fighter pilot who today helps Dad run the ranch. Bob, Jr., incidentally, preached frequently

18

at the ranch before he left for the mission field. Several hands were brought to Christ at his services.

Until recently the WHR boss did a bit of "preaching" of his own. He taught a boys' Sunday-school class in the First Presbyterian Church of Cheyenne, and one boy from the class is now preaching the gospel. Lazear was the first president of the initial Gideon camp in Wyoming and helped place Bibles in Cheyenne hotels and hospitals.

So, it is a rich life for Robert W. Lazear there on the peaceful, rolling prairies outside old Cheyenne. If he were not an humble man, he might be a bit proud: An estimated 30,000,000 pounds of beef eaten during the past year were a result of WHR, either directly or indirectly. He has a ranch that rivals Yellowstone as a show place and enough blue ribbons for a quilt and a suit of clothes. And he has had bulls that he would not take $100,000 for. But, Bob Lazear will tell you any day, that most satisfying of all, he has a personal relationship with the Lord Jesus Christ, the Prince of Life!

...she took a train ride...

2

Jo Peterson and
her Silent Missionaries

A CHICAGO WOMAN who rarely speaks into a microphone, and only occasionally appears before audiences, probably preaches more hours to more people than any other gospel messenger in the world. To do this, she does not have to leave her small office in Chicago's Loop. Even when she is at home, her messages are heard by millions—night and day! Her method? The Word of God in display advertising. Nearly 15 years ago she began making attractive posters proclaiming the Word of God and since then has been acquainting people in two hemispheres with the Bible. Her silent missionaries probably preach as many as 75 million hours every year!

It was in 1937 that Miss Jo Peterson was struck by inspiration while riding a Chicago L-train. Part-time artist and registrar at Austin Evening School in Chicago, she idly read the colorful car cards advertising chewing gum, cigarettes, patent medicines, liquors and what not. Something for every need—except life's deeper needs.

Before she left the train she was planning an organization to advertise the Bible on L-trains and other public carriers.

21

Today her Best Seller Publicity, Inc., places thousands of attractive scripture posters each month in streetcars, busses, trains, ships, and in such other places as hospitals and factories. Work is done by home-town missionaries in more than 200 communities, and the same messages are expanded to billboard size or reduced to the dimensions of calling cards.

The car cards and scripture billboards have stopped many sinners in their tracks and literally put them on their knees. An Army colonel sped along the highway some months ago and was arrested—not by a policeman, but by the Holy Spirit as he read a portion of God's Word on a Best Seller billboard. It told him to seek the Lord, that judgment was coming. At first it "got on his nerves," but not long afterward he was on his knees and found Christ as personal Saviour. Likewise, a girl in Los Angeles became convicted of living far away from the Lord when she read: "Be not deceived; God is not mocked: for whatsoever a man soweth, that shall he also reap." One evening in a tent evangelistic service she recalled this accusing finger and surrendered to the Lord, "lock, stock and barrel."

Miss Peterson (christened Josephine) spent her formative years planning to be a foreign missionary. She taught Sunday school as a 12-year-old, and when she was 17 became instructor of an adult Bible class in Chicago's Trinity Methodist Church. Later, she worked her way through Wheaton College in Wheaton, Ill., then failed to pass her physical for the mission field and began studying art.

Finally, in 1937 she took her memorable train ride. After much prayer, and fully convinced that her Best Seller idea was of the Lord, Miss Peterson went door-knocking. A few years earlier she had visited Europe to study art and had rapped at doors of several old world masters. Now, on more serious business, she laid her plan before Vaughn Shoemaker, Pulitzer prize-winner and chief cartoonist for the Chicago *Daily News;* Francis Chase, designer and magazine-cover artist; and Warner Sallman, whose "Head of Christ" painting is known to millions. Each volunteered to supply the artistic ability needed to launch her program. They would give her religious posters professional sparkle.

Like more than 400 other volunteer workers who help produce and distribute the posters and billboards, these established commercial artists serve without pay. Miss Peterson quit her school job to become full-time executive secretary of BSP after working as a volunteer for eight years. She and a secretary-steno are the only paid workers and their salaries are modest.

Contributions come from Christians wherever the work is known, and may be as little as 50 cents or as much as $1,000. One donor sends small amounts regularly from a county home for the aged; once a woman gave the money she had saved to pay off a mortgage. In Los Angeles, where more than 1,000 placards are displayed, two small boys, Jimmy and Jerry, heard the story of the scripture cards from their Sunday-school teacher, and at once pledged their chore money of $1 a month. Later, they organized a neighborhood club called Poster Partners, and raised $5.70 at their initial meeting. Poster Partners, an idea which has spread to other cities, urges members to keep a BSP card over their beds as a prayer reminder.

The original contribution to BSP was $40, from Dr. J. L. McLaughlin, secretary of the American Bible Society; this went for postage to announce the project. The name Best Seller Publicity, chosen because the Bible outsells all other books, was decided upon at a dinner sponsored by the late Mrs. Philip D. Armour, wife of the meat packer.

First car cards were posted in February 1938 in 240 Chicago streetcars; since then the number in Chicago has increased to a peak of 3,000, and the plan has caught on in scores of other cities every year. Local committees obtain cards from BSP headquarters and deal with advertising agencies for space. Many of the cards go up at reduced rates. In Los Angeles it is not unusual to see six or eight posters in a car, sometimes one in Spanish.

In a Canadian city Christian streetcar motormen themselves organized a committee, and in New York City, where about 1,000 cards are regularly displayed, a Columbia University professor helped launch the work. A 12-year-old boy heard about BSP on a radio broadcast and quickly got posters into busses in Elkhart, Indiana; he later moved and, with his father, began directing efforts in two Texas towns.

So, with millions daily reading Best Seller posters, it is little wonder that letters pour into headquarters telling of results. Miss Peterson will never forget the Jewish lawyer who read a poster in the bus in New York City. Unable to get away from the scripture, "I am the Resurrection and the Life . . .," he went to the New York office and listened intently to the Bible record of how his Messiah had come to make atonement for his sins. After repenting and coming into a personal relationship with Christ, the lawyer left saying, "This is the happiest half hour I have ever spent."

Jerry, a west-coast racketeer, wrote a card to BSP asking to see someone. A worker called at his apartment and listened to his story. Jerry, fed up and disgusted with life and nauseated with his underworld activities, wanted something that would satisfy. "I'd like one of those books you publish," he said. Explaining that Best Seller does not publish Bibles but only advertises the Word, the BSP volunteer gave Jerry a Testament, after marking the verses Jerry had memorized from the streetcar posters. He also accepted scripture cards which he posted in his apartment. Last report was that Jerry is telling his friends to put their trust in God and "that Man Jesus up above."

One letter told the story of a young man who read a placard on his way home from a night club. He had packed plenty of pleasure into his 20-odd years but nothing gave him lasting joy. On an L-train he read: "I am the Light of the world — Whosoever believeth in Me shall not walk in darkness but shall have the light of life."

The word *darkness* stood out to him. He was in *darkness*; things looked blacker to him each day. Fact is, he was in such *darkness* that he could face life no longer. Every day for a week as he rode to and from work, he looked for, and read, that poster. The words drove him into a rescue mission, and there he accepted Christ as Saviour. He says he is thankful for Best Seller placards because he came out of "*darkness* into His light."

Not long ago Miss Peterson told the Best Seller story in a school chapel meeting. Afterwards a young girl came up and excitedly announced, "I want to tell you what Best Seller posters did for me." Briefly, she had been "looking for a way to go," when the posters in the streetcars caught her attention. Impressed, she mentioned them to a fellow-worker, who invited her to her church. Result: she met the Lord and is now preparing for missionary service in India.

So, with proof that her idea is helping people to find the Bible, Miss Jo Peterson, whose headquarters are at 189 West Madison Street, Chicago, is extremely satisfied in her life work. Though seldom seen by the people to whom she preaches, her presentation of the message reaches millions. And as long as the Lord sends in the funds and as long as there are Christian artists and printing presses, her Best Seller Publicity committees will reach the straphanger with the good news, "Jesus Saves."

...apparently in good health...

3

The Real
Doctor Christian

THE SHARP RING of the telephone shattered the early morning silence. Dr. Walter L. Wilson, an almost bald, mustached physician, slipped from his bed and answered. A woman was ill, and would he please come. A few minutes later, the doctor's black sedan stopped in front of a small cottage on the outskirts of Kansas City, Mo.

Elderly and alone, the patient apologized for getting the doctor out before daylight, but she feared the worst if she waited longer. In routine fashion, Dr. Wilson took her temperature and pulse. Strangely enough, both were normal. Apparently she was in good health. So, on a hunch he asked gently, "Perhaps, Mrs. P——, you're afraid you'll die."

The patient stared at him a full moment, then burst into tears. "Yes, doctor, and I have been for years!"

With this new twist in the case, the kindly physician replaced his instruments in his medical bag and withdrew a small leather-bound Bible. He read to her how Jesus had come to open heaven's door to everyone who would open his heart's door to Him. Soon, the patient asked Christ to purge her of her sins and enter her life.

Later that same morning Dr. Wilson got a call from a neighbor of the patient. "Mrs. P—— is fully recovered. She had her wash out before nine and I can hear her singing from here . . ."

Recalling this and scores of other similar experiences during his career of half a century, Dr. Wilson declares that often illness is a direct result of "soul trouble" and salvation brings an immediate cure. And because he believes so strongly in salvation for every individual, whether unhealthy or healthy, the slight-built, 70-year-old Kansas City M.D., spends as little time as possible doctoring physical ailments and devotes most of his time prescribing the Lord Jesus Christ for sin-cursed hearts that beat in every human breast. He travels as many as 25,000 miles annually to preach the gospel and over the years has spoken in every state except South Dakota, Utah and Nevada. His year's itinerary includes service clubs, schools and churches of nearly every Protestant denomination. As a result, he is America's best known physician-minister.

He is equally as skillful in handling an audience as he is in treating a baffling medical case. Gentle and understanding, he is adept in pulling just the right illustration from his repertory of stories from days gone by, stories that will catch the ear of a fidgety schoolboy or even a preoccupied business executive.

Once at a Lions Club gathering in one of America's largest cities, Dr. Wilson faced a noisy group who apparently were not keen on listening to an expected sermon. The doctor asked God for special wisdom and stepped to the rostrum. He began with a story of his "old friend, Buffalo Bill," and suddenly had perfect attention.

His visit with the famous showman occurred in William F. Cody's private tent, designed especially for him by the tent company which Dr. Wilson represented in the old days. "I went into his tent to go over details of the show," the physician told the Lions. "At the close of the conversation, I asked him where he expected to spend eternity. Colonel William F. Cody [Buffalo Bill], indicated he was not concerned. 'My idea of real joy,' he boasted, 'is to have my cowboys dig a water hole in the middle of the arena, and fill it with water. Then I dip my ten-gallon hat into it, and let my horse drink first, after which I bury my face in the hat and drink. When 17,000 people cheer at the top of their voices, that's my idea of heaven.' "

With that beginning, Dr. Wilson had no trouble in making his application concerning what the Bible has to say about who will spend eternity where. At the close, a brigadier general came to Dr. Wilson, having been deeply moved by the gospel. To climax the meeting, he gave the doctor his hand and Christ his heart.

Today, at the scriptural age of three score years and ten, Dr. Wilson still talks of Buffalo Bill and days with the tent company as though it were yesterday. And in some respects, he looks much as though he stepped out of yesterday, perhaps from the family doctor's office of a western town. Always impeccably dressed, he wears big, light-colored hats that whisper of the West, and when removed reveal white hair that curls back slightly at the sides. Laughing blue eyes, a trim mustache, and a gold watch chain dangling from his pocket add to the touch of yesterday's typical family physician.

So, it is natural that students especially would be drawn to him. His messages interspersed with home-spun philosophy have been the means of scores of students, and even principals and teachers finding Christ. However, here and there he runs into a problem student that requires special attention. For instance, before a school chapel meeting some years ago, Dr. Wilson was approached by a 17-year-old senior. Cynically, he asked, "Are you the preacher that's supposed to preach this morning?"

"Yes," Dr. Wilson replied. "I plan to talk of some interesting things which perhaps you will enjoy."

"More than likely I won't," he said, "because I don't believe the 'bunk' that you preachers put out."

"Well!" the doctor exclaimed, "*that* is interesting. Now that you have told me what you do not believe, perhaps you might like to tell me what you *do* believe. I am far more interested in what you *do* believe than in what you *don't* believe."

"I will believe only what I can understand: none of that mystery stuff for me," he replied very emphatically. With that, the student went to his seat by the side of his redheaded sweetheart, and Dr. Wilson went to the platform.

"In your midst," he said during his talk, "you have a very wonderful young man. He is, of course, a senior. A senior is one who knows everything, and knows that he knows everything. He has just told me that he believed nothing that he could not understand. So I will ask this young gentleman if he will please explain to the audience how it is that a black cow eats green grass, which makes white milk, and churns yellow butter, and makes red hair on his sweetheart's head, when she partakes of it."

The laughter throughout the building was soon changed to deep thinking, as the students realized that many things in life must be taken by faith, and that explanation is not always possible. The senior and the redhead listened attentively to the address which lasted for one and a half hours. Throughout the lecture there was a constant comparison made between the miracles of the Lord seen in nature and the miracles recorded in the Bible. He called attention to the remarkable transformation that takes place when a caterpillar ("upholstered worms," says Dr. Wilson humorously) encases itself in its home-made casket and is changed into a beautiful butterfly, with its crawling instinct changed into a flying instinct. "Thus," Dr. Wilson pointed out, "will God

30

take the life of a sinner and transform it, until it glows with the beauty of the Lord and is fragrant with the graces of heaven."

At the conclusion of the address, Dr. Wilson watched with disappointment as the senior left the auditorium. But he was overjoyed at what the principal said. "Doctor, I have been deeply impressed with the perfections of God. Will you tell me, please, how to find the Saviour this morning?" Tears welled in his eyes. "My life has had too many failures in it. I am going around in a circle and getting nowhere. I want the Lord to take charge of me today." After a short talk with Dr. Wilson the principal asked Christ to cleanse him and dwell within.

Dr. Walter Lewis Wilson was born May 27, 1881, at Aurora, Ill., and after his mother's death went as a two-year-old to live with his Grandmother Dyke and his Uncle Nathaniel Dyke in Fort Smith, Arkansas.

In 1889 he moved to Kansas City, his present home, to live with his father, a practicing physician, magician and ordained Methodist minister. Here he decided to follow in Dad's footsteps—to be both a preacher and physician. He was a 15-year-old paper carrier when he was born again, as a result of many nights of gospel services and realization of the true meaning of Colossians 2:14—"Blotting out the handwriting of ordinances that was against us, which was contrary to us, and took it out of the way, nailing it to his cross." Christ, he saw now, had taken away the curse of the law of the Old Testament and had provided salvation for *him* through His death on the cross.

Walter Wilson's first sermons were in the form of tracts he distributed with his newspapers. But when he was 17, he began preaching on the streets of Kansas City—which, incidentally, was the only seminary he ever attended. He, however, says today that he won no souls until he became yielded to the Holy Spirit fifteen years later. The Holy Spirit then began to touch hearts of individuals to whom he spoke.

After being graduated from high school, Walter Wilson studied medicine for four years at Kansas City Medical College and then took a year at Northwestern University to learn how to overcome the handicap of color-blindness.

Shortly after beginning his practice in Webb City, Mo., he had to go out of business. His father-in-law, C. J. Baker became ill and called his doctor son-in-law, then twenty-six, to take over his tent and awning company, later Baker-Lockwood Manufacturing Company, biggest distributors of awnings and tents. In the factory, Dr. Wilson directed work from his medical offices, at the same time acting as company physician, and carrying on charity- and other medical work in the Kansas City area.

He did extensive field work for the tent company and was highly respected by most showmen for his stand for Christ. On one occasion Dr. Wilson entered the "saloon car" of a circus train on a siding at Meridan, Miss. The owner was playing poker with employees. A gun lay on the table. Several other men were sitting at other tables, gambling and drinking. As the doctor stepped inside, the owner arose. "Put the stuff away, men. Here is Dr. Wilson with a Bible. None of this stuff should go on where there's a Bible." The group obeyed, and Dr. Wilson had the privilege of giving them a brief gospel message.

After leaving the tent business, the physician set up practice again in Kansas City and for 14 years taught down-to-earth Bible lessons each week-day morning over powerful Radio Station WDAF. His technique was as unique as it is today. A letter from a Colorado woman bears it out. She wrote that her boys were fussing over a pair of socks just as Dr. Wilson was introduced on the air one morning. "I wanted them to listen," her letter continued, "but the fuss continued. Just before beginning the lesson, you said, 'Now boys, stop that fussing over those socks—listen!' They suddenly became as meek as lambs. They've listened attentively every morning since."

Today, between speaking engagements and during spare time from his Central Bible Church in downtown Kansas City and task of directing the program at his Kansas City Bible College, the doctor occasionally takes time to turn out a book. At least two of his twenty books are approaching the million sales mark. They are *Romance of a Doctor's Visits* and *Miracles of a Doctor's Life*.

But all of the time, whether traveling or in Kansas City, he is carrying on a hobby taken up as a teen-ager. An aged preacher instilled a desire in Dr. Wilson to learn what goes on in the plant and animal kingdoms; so everywhere the physician goes he is on the lookout for interesting material. He carries scissors with him, clips papers and magazines as he reads. If he runs across an ad of a book on curious and odd subjects, he invests in the volume. He frequently browses in second-hand book stores and grabs out-of-print numbers for his collection.

As a result of his nature studies, Dr. Wilson can rattle off countless interesting bits. He can tell you almost anything —from the odd way a flea jumps to why a horse rises from the ground with its front legs first, a cow with its hind legs, and an elephant with four.

And in his clever, inimitable way, he seems to put all of his knowledge to work for the Lord at just the right time and place. And whether back in harness as a physician or speaking from a pulpit, he is one medical man who is concerned more about the spiritual ailments of people than the physical!

...reluctantly, he agreed to go...

4

They Called
Him "Lucky Lou"

Reason ONE: About 1919 in
Los Angeles a man awoke one night to find his house in
flames, and dashed out with his wife and two older children.
Then he returned for the baby boy, but in confusion rescued
a pillow instead. Outside, he saw his mistake, and dashed
back in again and pulled the baby from under the bed where
he had tumbled. Despite the fact the porch had collapsed,
he got out safely, the baby unharmed. The baby who narrowly escaped a fiery death was Louis Zamperini, later to
become an Olympic track star.

REASON TWO: In the early '20s two boys of kinder-
garten age staged a race across a boulevard. One boy won
the race by a stride—just enough to place him in front of
an onrushing car. The winner was killed instantly. The
loser, Lou Zamperini, escaped unhurt.

REASON THREE: In 1936 in Berlin, Germany, following the Olympic games, an American athlete scrambled up
a flagpole for Hitler's private Swastika, flying proudly above
the chancellery. Two guards rushed forward, each firing a
shot. When they reached the pole the American was down,

the Swastika under his arm. Later, a German general faced the American:

"What you have done is punishable by death in Germany! Why did you do it?"

Unruffled by the incident, the American quickly soothed the general's feelings: "I wanted it, sir, to remind me of the wonderful time I've had here in Germany!" The American, the first United States runner to finish in the 5000 meter race, was Lou Zamperini, a high-school boy from California. One radio commentator solemnly told the nation that this act almost caused an "international incident."

REASON FOUR: During World War II in the South Pacific a B-24 crashed into the ocean, killing all but three of 11 crewmen. Two of the survivors (the third did not hold out) lived 47 days on a life raft, then spent 43 days in solitary confinement and 28 months in a Japanese prison. The two men: Pilot Capt. Russell Phillips and Capt. Lou Zamperini, the bombardier.

Because of these and other close brushes with death, Zamperini, track sensation* of the late '30s at the University of Southern California, was known for years as "Lucky Lou." Boyhood friends told him he must have been born under a lucky star. Lou believed it, too—that is, *until a few years ago.* And, oddly enough, he started to sour on the nickname *during* his amazing experience and deliverance in the Pacific! As a result, today Lou Zamperini no longer believes in "luck." "Lucky Lou" is a name of history.

Because of the change he does not jingle as much money as he otherwise would. A booking agency offered him $50,000 annually to tell his gripping raft story to audiences over America, a war story rated by some newsmen as second only to the atomic bomb. But since it developed that luck had

---

* In 1938 Zamperini set the national collegiate record for the outdoor mile at 4.8.3. In 1940 he set the ICCA record at 4.11. Earlier, in 1934, he broke the world's interscholastic mile record. All but the ICAA record still stand.

nothing to do with it, that all honor would now have to go to the Lord . . . well, the booking agency was no longer interested. Lou had suddenly become too religious.

How Zamperini, at the age of 32, came face to face with God is a story that has stirred thousands. For since his personal encounter with the Lord Jesus Christ, wiry, lean Lou has spoken from coast to coast, to church congregations, youth rallies, and other gatherings, and has even journeyed to Japan—a land he swore he would never look upon again—to tell how new life suddenly became his.

The change in Zamperini and his new outlook on life came in the fall of '49, when things looked especially dark for him. For five years following his return from the war he had struggled through a series of financial setbacks, beginning when two associates skipped the country with all of his GI earnings. The one bright spot in life was Cynthia, a beautiful brunette and formerly one of Florida's leading debutantes whom he married in 1946 following a whirlwind romance. And now in the fall of '49 he came dangerously close to losing her:

A Mexican government official came to the Zamperini's home in Los Angeles to discuss a proposition which would make Zamperini Mexico's hunting- and fishing-license agent in the United States. Cynthia Zamperini decided to ride to Mexico with the official to await Lou's later arrival, but changed her plans at the last minute. The official, who boasted of being an expert driver that needed no insurance, was killed in a crash on the return trip. Had Cynthia gone, she, too, probably would have died, so horrible was the accident.

But that night found Cynthia safe and comfortable in a revival tent in downtown Los Angeles. Billy Graham, the dynamic North Carolina evangelist, was in the midst of a campaign that had catapulted him to national fame, and she had gone out of curiosity to hear a fellow Southerner. That night her curiosity paid off in eternal values as she was convicted of sin, repented, and trusted Christ as her personal Saviour.

This, as it turned out, was the beginning of Zamperini's own miracle. She urged him to attend a Graham meeting, but husband Lou, who had not been to church for twelve years since he lost interest in the Roman Catholic Church, stubbornly refused. So Cynthia tried other tactics, pointing out that Graham was not really so dull, that he talked about scads of interesting things, including world and scientific facts. Reluctantly, Zamperini agreed to go, and on Sunday night, October 15, shouldered his way through expectant crowds and plopped himself on a bench. That night nothing happened and he left before the meeting was over. However, the following night he returned, despite the fact he had intended going to a movie; this time he sat spellbound through a message on the reality of hell.

As Graham urged people to get right with God, Zamperini delayed taking the step, believing that God would expect him to live a flawless life. God gave His answer when Billy Graham explained from the platform that, although true faith *leads* one to live a godly life, all Christians are imperfect in this life and find favor in God's sight only because of their faith relationship to Christ.

Something clicked inside the lean, wiry man's heart. And only seconds before Graham closed the night's meeting, Lou Zamperini, the ex-track star, began the most important race of his life, a race that meant Life if he ran it, death if he did not . . . a race that took him to the altar where he asked Christ to receive him and purge him from sin and give him new desires to replace old ones. And in an instant it happened—a sinner transformed into a living saint!

That, in Lou Zamperini's mind, is the greatest miracle that has happened to him. Next day God led him to turn down a $20,000-a-year-liquor-selling job he had been banking on, and as the weeks passed he found taste for the "old things" disappearing. For instance, champagne no longer appealed to him.

Naturally, with this change so much a part of him, Lou quickly recognized that he would have to make drastic changes in his war story; the Lord now would be receiving the glory for his remarkable deliverance. Even the $50,000 offer from the booking agency would not convince him otherwise. "I wasn't a true Christian at the time of the Pacific experience, but I know God spared me for a purpose; it had to be more than luck," he declares. The story of the B-24 plane crash and other incidents which followed bear out Zamperini's statement:

When the big plane nosed down into the open sea, it exploded. Zamperini, hopelessly pinned beneath the tripod of a machine-gun mount inside the fast sinking plane, blacked out at about 50 feet. However, the next thing he knew he was free and floating upward toward a tangle of wires. Suddenly his Southern California class ring caught on an open window and he managed to pull himself through the window. Inflating his life jacket, he shot to the surface and climbed aboard with Pilot Phillips and Mac, the tailgunner, the only other survivors.

During their first two weeks the survivors learned to live on birds and fish. An albatross became their first victim, but after peeling back the skin, they gave up because of the sickening stench. Later, after nauseating attempts, they ate a fourth bird, and the third fish. Raft equipment included hooks and string, but sharks soon wrecked all their hooks.

A God-wrought miracle came on the thirteenth day. With lips swollen and throats parched, the drifters spotted a small black cloud. Rowing toward it, they soon despaired and Lou prayed the best he knew how. Soon, as they watched breathlessly, the cloud traveled over them, showering cooling waters on the little raft, enough for several days.

Lou points out that it would be miracle enough for the cloud merely to have passed over their small raft, but to shower rain, that was something else! Similar miracles were repeated several times.

On the 27th day, when the trio tied Capt. Eddie Rickenbacker's endurance record, they spotted a plane and took hope. Sending up a flare, they waited expectantly as the plane turned and came closer. Then their hearts stopped: the plane bore the familiar red circle of the enemy! For the next 90 minutes they lived in terror as the Japanese plane strafed the little raft, its three machine guns blazing death.

At last the would-be killer made a futile attempt with a bomb, then turned and disappeared in the distance. Zamperini, who spent the 90 minutes in the water, climbed back on the raft to discover that his two buddies were unharmed, despite the fact that the raft itself was riddled with holes. They spent days afterward patching their craft.

Being weaker than his buddies Mac died on the 33rd day. On the 47th day, with hope and strength almost gone, Zamperini and Phillips spotted land. By now Lou weighed hardly 70 pounds, and was mostly bone; his lips were swollen and bleeding. Phillips had fared no better. On shore they could see coconut palms and banana trees. Now they would live in luxury as they regained their health.

But out of nowhere a Japanese patrol boat chugged up and hauled them aboard. For 43 days they were kept in solitary confinement, their bed a corral floor. Zamperini continued to pray to the God he did not know and got relief in an unusual way. The Lord, he says, sent a fever on both and they were hardly conscious enough to feel any pain.

Finally both men were placed aboard a ship bound for another prison camp. Here the fever left both men simultaneously. For a short time in camp, however, things looked even darker. A guard slugged Zamperini, sending blood trickling down his face. This attracted the attention of a young guard who secretly told him that he, too, was a Christian (believing that all Americans were Christians). So he became Zamperini's self-appointed personal body guard, and when Zamperini was once again mistreated, the other guard later got black eyes for his deed. The Christian guard and other friendly Japanese afterward risked their lives to see that Zamperini and his fellow prisoner were nourished back to health.

Back in the United States following his conversion to Christ, Lou Zamperini began to get the desire to return to Japan, although he had never wanted to see the place again. Missionary-evangelist Bob Pierce gave a missionary challenge in a service Zamperini attended and afterward he said he became filled with a "complete desire to go back to Japan and do what God wants me to do." Armed with pictures of the very men who practiced atrocities upon him, he spent some time in Japan in late 1950 and had the rare privilege of pushing through prison doors that even top-flight newsmen were unable to enter. Inmates were amazed that a former prisoner of war would journey so far to tell them the good news of salvation. Some expressed a sincere desire to follow Christ, and Zamperini, now back in the States working with juvenile delinquents, under Youth for Christ, is praying for them.

So, today the man who once was known as "Lucky Lou" continues to set a fast pace. Only he is not running for Southern California on a cinder path; rather as a blood-washed saint he is running for God!

"...*no man is sure of life*...."

5

Death Takes
a Trolley Ride

On the rainy afternoon of May 25, 1950, a crowded Chicago streetcar rammed a loaded gasoline truck, killing or fatally injuring thirty-four and sending at least thirty others to hospitals. It was the nation's worst tragedy involving street vehicles. Among the injured was Vernon Anderson, 34-year-old business manager of "Christian Life" magazine. Hoping that others might profit from his harrowing experience, Anderson related his story to the author of "Saints Alive." It appears as told by Vernon Anderson.

Honey, we've had rain on the South Side all afternoon and the underpass at 63rd and State is generally flooded after a downpour. So, tonight, if I were you, I'd take the I.C. home instead of the streetcar."

This bit of advice from my wife, Delphine, in a phone conversation late on the afternoon of May 25, 1950, didn't get any action on my part. The suggestion was a good one, but the Illinois Central train stop was too far from home— and I didn't have a raincoat. The streetcar would put me closer. So, about 6 o'clock I left the office and headed for State Street. I had no idea then that I would wish later that I had taken my wife's advice . . .

The rush hour was on; so I stepped back to let the first trolley pass—too crowded. The next car—No. 7078—also was jammed, but rather than delay, I squeezed in, paid the conductor, and edged my way toward the front. Here and there were people whom I had seen on other days, but no one that I knew well enough to speak to. So, as I stood midway between the front and the center door, my eyes scanned the row of ads on my side of the car. I don't remember any specifically, but there were the usual slogans, mostly outright lies, such as "They Satisfy" and "Life at its Best." Only a Best Seller Publicity poster offered the only real answer from God's Word.*

After standing for fifty blocks, I got an aisle seat next to a teen-age girl. As the new, streamlined "Green Hornet" trolley buzzed along, I glanced at my paper, then laid it on my lap. I was tired and chose rather to sit quietly and review the events of the day. At work that morning we had begun the day with our usual devotional period, looking to the Lord for guidance for the day. Work itself had been heavy, evidenced by the fact that I had homework with me— pay-roll records to check for the preceding year.

As we approached 63rd Street, I sensed that the car was going at a pretty fast clip to pass an intersection. But trolley schedules are tight, I knew, and motormen sometimes have to step it up. Then it happened . . .

The trolley lurched to the left and someone yelled "Look out!" There was a tremendous impact. I had no chance to brace myself. I was hurled from my seat, my back striking

---

* Luke 4:4 was verse of the month: "Man shall not live by bread alone, but by every word of God." However, the verse for April may have been still up: "God sent not His Son into the world to condemn the world; but that the world through Him might be saved." Anderson does not remember; Best Seller hopes it was the latter, John 3:17.

the seat across the aisle. I landed on my hands and knees. Instinctively, I got to my feet to keep from being trampled by people who already were rushing madly for the center and rear exits. As I rose, facing the front of the car, a tremendous explosion seemed to almost take my head off. Instantly flames rushed in and then literally engulfed the car.

Then, of course, I had no way of knowing what had happened. I was concerned only in getting out. But I later got this story:

As my wife had predicted, the afternoon's heavy rains had flooded the streetcar tracks under a spur of the New York Central just below 63rd. Consequently all southbound State Street trolleys were stopped, flagged onto a turnaround and then rerouted. Flagman Charles Kleim had already directed fifty or sixty other cars as he watched No. 7078—my car—approach. Behind him, as he waited to stop Motorman Paul Manning, a heavy tank truck, loaded with 8,000 gallons of gasoline, crawled north on State. The driver, Mel Wilson, had almost laid off work that day; he would rather have stayed home to celebrate his son's graduation from grammar school.

As the big truck approached, Flagman Kleim waved frantically; something was wrong! Didn't Manning see him? Didn't he know he could not make the switch at that speed? Kleim froze as the streetcar veered to the left at the switch and plowed into Wilson's truck. Flagman Kleim retreated as a blinding explosion followed, drenching the truck cab with fiery gasoline and making the inside of the trolley a roaring inferno. Both Wilson and Motorman Manning died instantly. Various and sundry reasons were given for the accident. Some blamed the motorman, others suggested that the flagman was at fault. Official investigations failed to uncover any satisfactory explanation. Probably Manning either did not see the flagman or believed that he was waving him through. I don't know and neither does anyone else.

Inside the trolley I reconciled myself to the fact that escape was impossible. Somehow I wasn't particularly fearful, although I sickened at the thought of burning to death. Flames roared about me—yet I knew I was ready to die.

I, of course, didn't have time to review the details in that moment, but one evening in November 1931 I had come into a personal relationship with the Lord. I was a sophomore in Morgan Park High and had been attending services at the Salvation Army hall on Chicago's South Side with my folks. But until that November evening I hadn't realized that I needed to receive Christ personally as my Saviour. That evening I sat spellbound as a young evangelist, Winfield Johnson, of the "Sunshine Duo" gospel team, told how God had saved him from sin, of how through the Lord Jesus Christ he had received eternal life. Somehow he made me want what he had. Presently, as the invitation was given in the typical Salvation Army way, Johnson came down into the audience and laid a hand on my shoulder. I responded and later at the altar asked Christ to take away my sins and promised to live for Him.

The assurance of salvation that Christ had put into my heart way back then held me in that awful moment when escape from the streetcar seemed impossible. However, at the same time, I prayed that a miracle would happen. I reached out toward a window, but pulled back: steel bars covered half the window and the opening at the top was too small for a man's body to pass through. The end had come.

At this moment a supernatural power seemed to direct me, for what I did from here on wasn't voluntary. Why God chose to get me out, I can't explain. Several other known Christians, including Motorman Manning, died. But I do know that God does all things perfectly. If He has special work for me, I'm ready to do it.

But back to the escape. The aisle was jammed; so I vaulted over seats toward the rear of the trolley. Reaching the rear, I glanced back and in that split second saw hungry flames take hold of a woman's hair as other passengers scrambled madly toward a door that never opened, their clothing already aflame.

Even in the rear of the car, the heat was so intense that I thought my own hair was burning and instinctively pulled my coat up for protection. Just then a man jumped through a small rear window. I followed, head first, and as I hit the cool air I felt like my whole body would explode, the temperature change being so marked. As I went through the window, my left leg caught inside the car and I dangled, head down, for a few seconds. I managed to wrench the leg free and fell to the street, on my back. Dazed, my eyes watering and my eyeballs seemingly on fire, I picked myself up and instinctively ran away from the car. About a hundred feet from the car, I glanced back and the entire street from one side to the other was a mass of flames. Near-by buildings were already beginning to burn. From a window in the trolley, a woman dangled like a human torch. Spectators dashed here and there, and others stared wild-eyed. All were unashamedly calling on God for help. Two minutes before it had been a normal spring evening; now it was a scene of death and panic.

I would have run on and on, but a Negro man grabbed me and gently shoved me into his old jalopy automobile, and, together with two other victims—a man and a woman—hurried to a near-by hospital.

At the hospital I called Delphine, wanting to reach her before she got radio reports. A neighbor drove her to the hospital and I went home following first-aid treatment and X-rays of my leg and back. I went to bed immediately, and when I was settled as comfortable as circumstances permitted, Delphine crept down beside the bed and we had an old-fashioned prayer meeting. We thanked God for providential deliverance and asked Him to comfort other victims and families of those who perished.

Many days passed at our home before things were back to anywhere near normal. Beverly, our three-and-a-half-year-old daughter, refused to come near me; I must have looked like a mummy, with all my bandages, for she would stand off and stare wonderingly and say nothing. Little one-year-old Kurt, however, didn't notice the difference; he oo-ed and goo-ed as usual.

I didn't go to work for about two months, my injuries being worse than I had at first thought. A blood clot formed in my left leg and a strained back turned out to be a spinal injury. Even now, I'm still pretty much crippled up and for a long time was able to work only half a day.

For many nights following the tragedy I slept little. When darkness would fall the fiery streetcar came to haunt me with its wild-eyed victims, their hair and clothing aflame, screaming and dying. When I started out for work two months later, I took a streetcar but had to get off after only a few blocks, sick to my stomach for this same scene loomed before me.

Now, as I say, I'm back at work trying to get back into the swing of a normal life. Looking back, I realize more than ever what a thin thread life is hung on. It's like Job said: "Man that is born of a woman is of few days, and full of trouble." And later, ". . . no man is sure of life."

Another thing, the accident has given me many opportunities to witness of the importance of knowing Christ as personal Saviour. Several men, among them vendors whom I have contact with through business, have seemingly become concerned about the welfare of their souls. From my experience, they realize more clearly that life is uncertain, even for a man in the best of health. Their only hope for salvation, I have told them, is a personal acceptance of the Lord Jesus

Christ as Saviour. Some of them, I know, are thinking about this need, and one of these days I believe the harvest will come. Even if one soul comes to Christ as a result of my horrifying experience, the suffering would be worth it. After all, didn't Christ suffer for me that I might have life?

...steam can't stay in the kettle...

6

Joe of Joe's Place

W<small>ITH TWO OTHER MEN,</small> I was en route from Chicago to the East where I planned to interview several personalities for *Power*. Having left Chicago in the late afternoon, we began looking for an inviting restaurant as dusk fell upon the green farmlands of Indiana. A mile west of Wanatah, Indiana, as our big De Soto zoomed over the main street of America—the east-west Lincoln Highway—we spotted a green and red neon sign up ahead: "Eat— Joe's Place." Our driver had a hazy recollection of having met a man named Joe who had a restaurant somewhere on No. 30—a born-again Christian, he thought.

So we drove in at Joe's Place and parked. A moment later a stocky barrel-chested, thick-necked man with close-cut graying hair, came over to our car, his green sport shirt hanging loose. To test him, I handed him a colorfully wrapped tract, called a gospel bomb.

Immediately his face brightened up. "Say! it's a tract. Praise the Lord!" And with that he greeted us like lost brothers.

Inside, I learned his name was Joe Clifford, that he and

his wife, Mabel, a quiet blonde who spends much of her time in the kitchen, had operated their combination gas station and roadside cafe for about five years. They prayed to get the land, his wife said, managing to buy it despite the fact the owner's brother-in-law had wanted it for years. The place is a two-story frame structure, with a dazzling flower garden in the back yard. Joe and his wife live in the two up-stairs rooms and work in the tiny kitchen and cafe which has four tables and a lunch counter.

Inside and out, the place is neat and spotless, the kind of cafe your heart and stomach like when you're in strange sur-roundings and have to grab a bite on the run. Just inside the door there's a sign: "Closed Sundays." On the wall behind the lunch counter are two tiny plaques. One is "Jesus Saves" and the other, "Thy Word have I hid in my heart." I noticed a Bible behind the counter.

And after talking to Joe Clifford I had no doubt that God's Word is his favorite food. Physically, he's stacked up like a pro football lineman—215 pounds of brawn; hairy, muscular arms, and a square chin. But spiritually he's even more robust. He believes "if there's steam in the kettle, it's got to come out." He follows the advice Paul gave Timothy in II Timothy: ". . . preach the Word, dwelling on it con-tinually, welcome or unwelcome" (from the Knox translation).

After Joe had served our table that evening, two plainly dressed men with heavy black beards ambled in and seated themselves at the lunch counter. Obviously, they were Amish and supposedly Christians. One selected a gospel tract from a container on the counter after giving his order. Soon Joe stepped up and asked, "Are you fellers born-again Christians —do you know Christ as your personal Saviour?"

Apparently caught off guard, one of the good men mum-bled that they thought so, "hope so and aim to be."

It wasn't a very good answer and Joe quickly let them know it. He emphasized it pointedly, adding that the Bible makes it clear in such passages as I John 5:13 that anyone can know for sure that salvation is his.

When the men arose to resume their journey, one asked for several extra copies of the tract, which Joe himself authored three years ago. It seemed that they were leaving to do a bit of witnessing of their own. The man whose answer had set off Joe a few moments before thanked Joe, adding that they were glad they had stopped in. "We thank the Lord for taking us to such a nice clean place."

Joe's Place, with its good food and homey surroundings, is the type of roadside restaurant you'd expect would be a regular stop for truck drivers. But only six stop with any regularity; all are family men, Joe says. The others who have stopped haven't returned, for they apparently prefer jukeboxes to Joe and the gospel.

Joe especially remembers one big truck driver, the first customer one morning, who came in bleary-eyed from the long grind, and challenged Joe to put up his dukes and step outside to take him down a peg or two. "Listen, friend," Joe said, eyeing him unflinchingly, "when a fellow is a Christian he doesn't want to fight." Still the trucker insisted that Joe needed a whipping. So Joe cut in. "We're not getting anywhere, so let's drop it. Anyhow, my Bible tells me this is a case of 'casting my pearls before swine.'"

Commenting on the incident, Joe remarked, "Before I was saved I would have been delighted to have stepped outside!"

Mrs. Clifford had already hinted that Joe was a bad one in days gone by. "I prayed eight years for his salvation," she said simply. "We couldn't have lived together after he returned from service if he hadn't come back changed."

Joe joined the Navy at thirty-five in the early days of the war and soon was helping train other Seabees to operate huge shovels and cranes in the New Hebrides in the South Pacific. Here Joe began to get serious about life. The chaplain had already launched a back-to-the-Bible campaign, so Joe began reading his New Testament. "I was a Catholic and plenty religious," Joe remarked, "but I soon saw I needed to be saved." So later, in the Admiralties, Joe, the Seabee, opened his heart to the Lord Jesus Christ, trusting Christ's atoning work on Calvary for his soul's redemption.

Joe had no doubt but that salvation is real, for it began affecting his way of living. God was real to him now. Soon after, he came down with malaria and put God to a test. "I was so sick I went to sick bay," he recalls. "They gave me nothing but aspirin, and I remember praying to God to make me either so sick that they'd have to do something, or else for Him to heal me. Next day I was healed." Joe's faith is just as simple as that.

Today big Joe Clifford, the ex-Seabee, bubbles over with quotations from Scripture that are appropriate for every need. Asked the state of his business, he said, "I have food and raiment, and God tells us therewith to be content." This bright uplook makes it possible for Joe to be a real friend to the man on the Lincoln Highway.

A young man dropped onto a stool at the lunch counter, extremely downcast. Joe sought to help and learned that the traveler had just been swindled of $125, and hated to face his wife whom he was on his way to pick up in Pittsburgh. Joe quickly brought joy to the man's heart as he pointed him to the God of all comfort. Three hours later Joe went into the little Indiana town of Wanatah and passed the man sitting in his car; he was reading the New Testament.

Joe's fervency to reach the unsaved has not had any decided effect on his trade since most of his clientele are transients. But generally they return if they live in the vicinity, even if they left the first time hot under the collar. A new preacher in the neighborhood dropped in and Joe, no regarder of persons, put the question to him: "Are you born again, sir?"

"Why, I'll have you know I'm a preacher!" he exploded, naming a prominent denomination with which he was connected.

But Joe didn't bat an eye. "Yes, I know. But the thing that counts is whether you're born again."

The pastor left hurriedly, but returned two weeks later to apologize. He admitted he had given a poor answer and assured Joe that he did know Christ as his personal Saviour.

A candy salesman calls regularly at Joe's Place. Claiming to be an atheist, he insisted he was so mean that even if there was a God, He wouldn't have anything to do with him. But things are different now: "Today," Joe wrote me some weeks after my visit, "if you were to meet the candy salesman he could testify to knowing the Lord Jesus Christ as his personal Saviour, having found the way to eternal life through his delivering candy and gum once a week and hearing the gospel preached here many times (Isa. 55:10,11)."

Generally, the people at Joe's are new faces. They are travelers from the West and East, and the North and the South—tall and short, fat and thin—people who are sad—all with varying philosophies of life. But the strangest of them all was a group that had formed a religion all their own, from the "good" points of several satanic cults. Another odd character tried to sell Joe on reincarnation of the human spirit. He believed he was living on earth for the third time, had once been a rooster and before that, a cow.

Thus the Joe Cliffords have a never-ending task of getting the gospel into the hands and hearts of the confused and spiritually blind people who travel the main street of America, the Lincoln Highway. And they're getting a lot of fun out of doing it, as they work and live in their place beside the road.

"...nothin' 'igh 'at..."

7

Meet
Alberta's Premier

*as told by Don Peacock, and written
in collaboration with the author*

I LIVED IN ALBERTA—one of Canada's western provinces—until I was graduated from high school in 1948. From the time I was old enough to know that premiers run provincial governments—much like governors do the forty-eight states—I thought premiers were members of a special set of people. Now I know otherwise.

My illusion came to an abrupt end as a result of an assignment from *Power* to interview Premier Ernest C. Manning, who began his second full term as chief executive in Alberta in the fall of 1948. I followed this election from the States, where I was in school at the time.

When I got off the ancient trolley in Edmonton and walked up to the domed capital of Alberta, I realized I was early for my appointment. So I struck up a conversation with a window washer. He was a friendly, middle-aged fellow and glad to find an excuse for a pause in his work. He told me that he had spoken to the Premier a few times in his long years around the parliament building and added in a noticeable English accent, "There's nothin' 'igh 'at about Premier Mannin'. 'E's just like talkin' to a ordinary guy."

Inside, however, one of his two secretaries impressed upon my mind the fact that he's more than an "ordinary guy": "I don't think I'd want the Premier's job at twice his salary," she commented as I waited to go in.

When I finally entered the Premier's blue-carpeted office in the parliament building, I found him to be much like the man the window washer had described: friendly and informal.

But the thing that impressed me most about this slim, bespectacled man in the dark blue suit was the way he talked so freely and familiarly about Christ and what He had done for him. I sensed, as I watched Premier Manning across his broad desk, that politics is not his primary interest.

"It may sound strange coming from me," he said, casting a thoughtful glance at the broad North Saskatchewan River which can be seen from his office window, "but as long as God sees fit to keep me in office as Premier of Alberta, it is my greatest hope that I may always use the prestige of my position to witness for Christ."

Those words, I think, explain more clearly than any of the various reasons given by political writers and commentators why Premier Manning has risen to his present position in so short a time. His popularity with Albertans has steadily grown since his first election, in 1935, to the Legislative Assembly. Last election, for instance, he himself pulled almost as many votes as the entire total received by his 21 opponents. Result: the Social Credit party that he leads scored its most sweeping victory ever.

Coming from a small Saskatchewan farm home where God's Word was honored and read daily, Premier Manning has a background that would seemingly least equip him for success as a politician. He has no college or university education—he was, however, graduated from the Prophetic Bible Institute in 1930.

Premier Manning cannot give the exact date of his conversion. He did, however, definitely receive the assurance of his salvation one Sunday afternoon in 1926 while at home listening to a radio broadcast by William Aberhart, then a high-school teacher in Calgary, Alberta.

A year later, at nineteen, he felt God calling him to Bible school. That fall he left his farm home in Saskatchewan and went to Calgary, where he was the first student to enroll in Aberhart's newly founded Prophetic Bible Institute. He soon began assisting Aberhart with the school's radio broadcasts and often accompanied him on speaking tours.

Ever since hearing that radio broadcast more than twenty years ago, Manning has tried to let God have complete control of his life. So it is not surprising that soon after entering Bible school, he began to find many doors of service open.

During his first summer at home between Bible school terms, he drove twenty miles every Sunday to teach a Bible class in a small country schoolhouse. In that time he built up the attendance from twenty to seventy. He continued a busy life of full-time Bible teaching and preaching until 1935.

That year the Social Credit party, organized by William Aberhart, ran in the Alberta election for the first time, and Manning took time out to make a few speeches as one of the party's nominees for the Calgary constituency. Result: he easily won a seat in the Legislative Assembly. Soon after the election, William Aberhart, the new Social Credit Premier of Alberta, appointed him provincial secretary. At twenty-six he became the youngest cabinet minister in the British Empire!

Following the election the young politician moved to Edmonton and began his career as a lawmaker, working closely with Premier Aberhart at the job of governing Alberta. But he and the Premier were soon holding gospel radio services and other large meetings whenever their duties as statesmen permitted. Manning worked hard as a politician, but he worked just as hard at telling others about Christ.

When Premier Aberhart died in 1943, Manning, at thirty-five, was the logical choice of his fellow Social Creditors to become Aberhart's successor. He also took over duties as president of the Prophetic Bible Institute.

Today the Premier and his wife conduct regular Sunday radio services from the Institute, their evening "Back to the Bible Hour" now covering most of western Canada and reaching into the United States. In other spare time Premier Manning speaks at gospel rallies, conferences, special meetings and any other place in which he feels God can use him.

As the Premier continued to answer my questions in his simple, direct way, I asked him what effect his testimony had on the people he came in contact with in his various activities, in and out of the Province.

"In almost every instance," he answered, "I have found my testimony respected. People may not agree with my beliefs, but it's amazing how many respect them. I realize, of course," he continued, "that the dignity of my position may have something to do with that. But I believe that a whole lot of Christians get themselves into trouble by sitting on the fence instead of making their stand clear."

Because he does not sit on the fence, visitors sometimes remain in Premier Manning's office to discuss Christianity. He has had many opportunities to witness for Christ in this way. To illustrate, a Canadian newspaper writer was so impressed by Premier Manning's stand that he told all his friends about it when he returned home. Somehow his insistent claim that he had actually discovered a politician who was a real God-fearing, God-serving Christian found its way to the ears of the Christian Business Men's Committee in Chicago. Skeptical, the Chicago CBMC wrote Premier Manning to find out for themselves. The result: the Premier was asked to start a branch of the Committee in Edmonton. And he did.

The Edmonton CBMC branch has grown considerably. Its influence touches many lives. An Edmonton lawyer approached a member and asked him about salvation. "If Manning believes so strongly in this kind of Christianity," the lawyer concluded, "there must be something to it."

Not everyone, however, believes that Alberta's Premier is sincere about religious beliefs. A skeptical reporter, attempting to show that Manning's Sunday broadcasts were partly for political gain, wrote an article for English and Australian newspapers. But instead of damaging Manning's reputation, the article backfired: letters poured in from sympathetic Christians as well as curious doubters, and because every letter is carefully answered, the result was more opportunities to witness for Christ.

"The reporter almost gave the gospel himself," the Premier observed with a faint smile, "while trying to describe our broadcasts."

A moment later the telephone rang and Premier Manning was reminded that he had to be at a radio station within fifteen minutes. A short time later he and Mrs. Manning were scheduled to take a private plane for New Jersey, where Alberta's first lady would christen one of the latest additions to Canada's merchant navy.

I prepared to leave the big room and Premier Manning took my hand. His grip was firm and strong. "Well, I'm glad to have met you," he said, "and may the Lord bless you in the future." He offered to drive me uptown if I were going that way, but I wasn't.

When I was out of the parliament building and walking in the late afternoon sun toward the streetcar stop, I could still remember his final words. I felt more like a young man leaving the home of a close Christian friend than like a young writer who had interviewed Alberta's Premier.

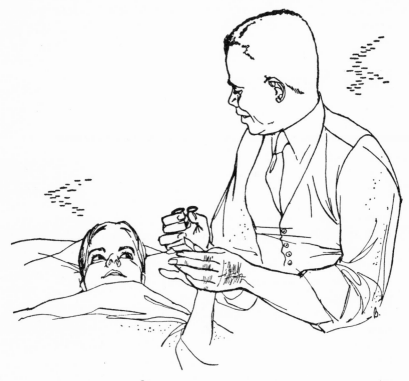

...his prescription works...

8

Dark Samaritan

It is two hours past midnight in a poor neighborhood on Chicago's near West Side. Upstairs in an apartment house a big Negro man slips from his bed; a moment later a light appears in the kitchen. The big man seats himself at the breakfast table where he opens a large worn Bible. For an hour he reads, his lips occasionally moving reverently.

Finally, he closes the Bible and slips back to his bedroom. But he does not return to bed. Instead he kneels by a big chair beside his bed. He calls it the Lord's chair. To him the Lord is more real than anything in the room; it is almost as if he could reach out and touch Him. For a long time the big man continues to pray, and if you would look closely you could see tear drops on the floor. The people he is praying for are very special; and they have great needs.

At last he arises, a brightness about his ebony face, and returns to bed to await the day.

This early morning quiet time is the secret of success in the ministry of Raymond Lilly, a 56-year-old ex-Arkansas farm boy, circus laborer, and steel-mill hand, who for a quarter of a century has worked for God among the patients in Cook County Hospital, Chicago, the largest charity institution of its kind on the North American continent. Although he seldom retires before 10 P.M. and is always up by 7:30, he finds his early morning time with the Lord far more necessary than extra sleep. It is the most important part of his ministry at the hospital, he says, although his labors in the institution itself have made him the hospital's best-known personality, loved and respected by staff members and patients alike. It is during his quiet time that he holds "those poor little things" (as he calls the patients) before the Lord and receives power for his ministry.

Lilly, a tall, graying 220-pounder who humbly refers to himself as "God's little servant," works 12 and 14 hours daily telling the gospel story while serving as manicurist and foot doctor and doing such other menial tasks as must be done, tasks that busy nurses rarely find time to do. In addition, he distributes among the patients many useful items: toothbrushes, razor blades, pencils, and combs, and bobby pins and hair nets for the ladies—each with a printed gospel message. To the patients—blacks, whites and yellows representing a cross section of poorer community life in the Windy City—it all adds up to a sermon that can not easily be brushed aside. For one thing, they can not doubt his sincerity, for he has never been paid for anything he does nor for anything he distributes.

Lilly, who in 1946 became the hospital's first official Negro chaplain, is used of the Holy Spirit to point more than 100 persons monthly to the Lord Jesus Christ. Many yield while ugly nails are being trimmed, others while aching limbs are being massaged by strong black fingers. Some open their hearts because he stops to sing a Negro spiritual or gospel song.

Doctors and nurses alike agree that Chaplain Lilly has the best prescription for bringing new life to the depressed and frightened, and for inspiring hope and courage in persons flat on their backs in a lonely world. Though his verbs may often be in the wrong tense and he may use a malapropism now and then, nobody notices it because Lilly's voice is soft and soothing, and you know his heart hurts for you when he stops by your bed.

Take the case of the automobile accident victim who landed in Ward 33, both legs broken, dejected and sick of living. His girl friend had been killed in the accident and he himself feared he would never use his legs again. To him, the world was more than dark; it had almost come to an end.

When Lilly heard his story, he suggested simply: "Now, my friend, my Jesus helped me and He wants to help you. But first, just tell Him you're a sinner and trust Him as your Lord and Saviour. Then we'll ask Him about your legs."

Soon a miracle took place. The power of the living Christ invaded the young man's heart and life, dispelling the gloom. Lilly prayed a simple prayer asking God to restore him to health. Later, he visited the man at home, prayed with him and massaged his legs. The last time Lilly heard from the man he was "using his legs for Jesus" on a government job.

Lilly's most unusual toenail case was 85-year-old William Woods, a Negro whom he met in April 1947, in a dimly lit hallway at County. Without slippers or shoes, Woods, a newly arrived patient, was making his way slowly to the washroom.

"Pardon me, sir," greeted Lilly gently, "but what is that noise I hears?" With each step the old man took, an odd, clomping sound echoed dully through the hallway.

Pointing helplessly to his bare feet, the patient said: "It's my toenails; ain't had nobody to cut them for me."

By this time Lilly was on his knees, examining the toenails, which were two or three inches long, thick and twisted

65

like billy goat horns. For 12 years the old man had lived alone, unable to care for himself because of partial paralysis. For four years, until he came to County, he had worn boat-like rubbers, the ends stuffed with paper to protect his toes.

Now I, too, would have been skeptical of such a story, but I watched Raymond Lilly start an operation on those unsightly nails. A girl social-worker earlier had attempted to cut them, but the job proved too difficult for her. Lilly completed them in less than an hour. While dressing the toes, he sang, "There is a Fountain Filled With Blood" and soon found that the patient, too, knew the song. Woods confessed that he once knew the Lord, and now wanted to live for Him. Today, living in a home for the aged, he maintains a ringing Christian testimony, reports Lilly, who has visited him on several occasions.

Raymond Lilly has always had a hankering to be with people, to be in places teeming with human excitement. Born 56 years ago into an Arkansas farm family of 12 children, he left home as a teen-ager to work with a railroad section gang, then joined Golmar Brothers Circus as a trapeze rigging man.

Later he went to a better job in a steel mill in Evanston, Illinois, and here worked with a kindly old janitor who had met God and was to be one of the Holy Spirit's instruments for reaching Lilly. One day the janitor said, "You ought to start making your life count for something, Raymond."

Lilly laughed. He was doing all right, he boasted. He was sowing a few wild oats, sure, but he was making out.

"But, Raymond, you're restless. And you'll admit you're not really happy down inside. Why not come around to our little mission some night and get fixed up with the Lord?"

Lilly said maybe, but it was his wife, Roberta, who accepted the invitation and was ultimately saved. This soon upset the Lilly household. Resentment toward the gospel grew in Lilly's heart, until one evening he pushed aside his unfinished meal and struck out for the mission to get even with the preacher who had put crazy ideas in his wife's head. With a brick in his hand ("and a stone in my heart," says Lilly), he looked for a window to smash. But a kindly woman saved the situation by cornering him and shaming him out of the idea. Soon Lilly found himself inside the mission hearing the gospel explained in detail. But he did not surrender without a fight; until the early morning hours he held on to his sins. Finally about 3 o'clock the struggle ended. Christ saved Raymond Lilly.

Soon Lilly began praying that the Lord would open a field of service for him. His answer came in 1926 when he called at Cook County Hospital to visit a sister who was a patient. After a brief chat he began a little exploration trip and was shocked when he looked into Wards 33 and 34, where male fracture cases lay. Many of the patients had shaggy beards and long, unkempt hair. Immediately the Holy Spirit seemed to speak. As a boy Lilly had trimmed the hair of his brothers, so why not serve men who could not afford barber work and give them the gospel while he worked on them?

Next day he returned with a cheap pair of clippers and a barber's razor and set to work. One hard-boiled nurse chased him out, but apologized profusely next day after she learned he was not just another fellow doing penance. For years Lilly cut hair and shaved hundreds of penniless patients, working just enough at odd jobs to keep things going at home. During the depression years of the '30s he sometimes walked the 70 blocks from his home for want of streetcar fare. That was how burdened he was for souls!

Lilly has had to adjust his techniques from time to time as circumstances required. Whereas his ministry began with free haircuts and shaves, he quit barbering several years ago to avoid trouble with union barbers. So today when he runs across an unusual case where something has to be done, he digs down into his pockets and personally pays to have the work done. Often this paves the way for Christ to come into another life. Other duties have replaced the barber work.

During most of his years at the hospital, Lilly has worked part time to pay bills both at home and at the hospital. But today his is a full-time ministry and is supported by gifts from God's people. After reading about Lilly's work more than four years ago, a missionary in the Far East began sending $10 regularly for supplies. Not long ago the National Association of Evangelicals decided to aid him up to a certain point if gifts failed to come in. But gifts usually come in, a dollar today and five tomorrow, as God touches the hearts of Christians who have heard about and are praying for Lilly's work of faith. Funds come marked for various purposes: "for tooth brushes," "for Gospels of John," or perhaps occasionally, "for personal use only."

I watched Chaplain Raymond Lilly in action at County. He knocked off work about 8 P.M. and we strolled along a corridor to his little office, where he prepared to leave for home. But two Christian women entered to visit patients and next thing I knew a prayer meeting was on. Lilly prayed for the contacts the women would make, for the many he had made during the day, and for the patients who would soon undergo surgery. He called them all by name.

"We praise Thee, Lord," he continued, "that when the saints go marching in, thousands will go up from old County Hospital and from the streets of wicked old Chicago because You let us talk to them about their dear souls." When he lifted his head tears glistened on his black cheeks.

We left his tiny office and headed toward a restaurant for a snack. I was hungry and was glad that Lilly was at last calling it a day. But at the door he spotted a doctor's chauffeur for whom he had been praying, and hurried to talk to him about his soul. Though plenty hungry I waited patiently, convinced that soul-winning is a full-time business with Raymond Lilly, the dark Samaritan of Cook County Hospital.

"...it's the reality I've found ..."

The Girl Who
Wore Blue Jeans

ISAAC C. ELSTON High School in
Michigan City, Indiana, was nearly deserted that gloomy
Saturday afternoon in May 1945. In only one of the rooms
of the yellow brick, block-long building was there activity.
Here a dozen or so jazz band enthusiasts were practicing for
their next dance engagement.

Finally, rehearsal over, the gang broke up, leaving only
a handful of stragglers who could not decide what to do or
where to go. One was Val Fluegge, the dreamy, blue-eyed
blonde songstress who had come to practice wearing jeans and
a red shirt. What could she do? Go home and play popular
records, or window-shop in the business district a few blocks
away? Suddenly she got an idea . . .

The school auditorium was being decorated for an
evening meeting—a large sign a man was bringing in
announced "Youth for Christ." Val dared herself to go.

That evening, still looking the part of a typical bobby-
soxer in her blue jeans, she slipped into the back row. The
singers seemed sincere and Val was impressed: she herself
had been called a "sincere" singer—but sometimes she

wondered. Who could be sincere singing the "Shoo-fly-pie" and "Whistler's Mother-in-law"?

She sat up a bit straighter as Billy Graham, the fiery, curly-haired youth speaker, who in 1945 was just starting out as an evangelist, gave a straight-from-the-shoulder gospel message. As the congregation sang a hymn, Val, unmindful of her blue jeans, hurried down the aisle and knelt at the front. There she told the Lord she wanted Him more than anything else in the world; jazz bands and all that went with them did not satisfy, and from this time on the Lord Jesus Christ would have her life and use it in His own way.

A few people may have smiled at the girl in blue jeans that night and others may have passed her off as just another teen-ager going through a growing-up stage. But that simple act and the decision that went with it changed the whole course of Val's life. At the age of 15, in Chicago she had earned spending money modeling on Saturdays and after school; in high school in Michigan City she was the sweetheart of the jazz band. Today, more than six years later? She is planning on foreign missionary service. Before this book was published, she wrote: ". . . I met one Norman Mydske of Seattle, Washington. The Lord has led us along separate paths these four and a half years since we met. . . . Norman is at present graduating from the BIOLA School of Missionary Medicine in Los Angeles. We plan to be married. . . . The Lord has called us both to missionary work. . . ."

This, however, won't be Val's first experience as a missionary. She started out almost immediately, beginning at home. First, her changed life caused her mother, who had been up to then a luke-warm Christian, to take a clear-cut stand for the Lord, making it known publicly at a morning church service.

But bespectacled Henry Fluegge, the father, was not to

be influenced so easily. Religion was out of his line; a musician, he had been traveling with vaudeville and other road shows as a pianist for years, almost since he played in his first concert at the age of five.

During the summer of '45, Henry Fluegge was filling a long engagement as pianist at Colosimo's Coliseum in Chicago. And at the same time a six-week evangelistic campaign was attracting the rest of the Fluegge family. More than anything else, Val wanted her dad to come so that he would hear the gospel and get what she had. She met with the evangelist for more than a score of pre-service prayer meetings just to pray for Dad. Then, during the final week of the campaign, Henry Fluegge took a night off from the entertainment world and went to the meeting to see what it was all about. And at the conclusion of the service he opened his heart to Christ.

Later, Fluegge got three wires from Sonja Henie to return as pianist for her Ice Revue show for which he played during the 1944-45 season. But he wasn't moved. Today he teaches piano and directs the choir for a Michigan City church. Mrs. Fluegge sings in the choir and teaches Sunday school. And Val, for one, is plenty happy about the whole thing.

These are just a few miracles in the life of Val Fluegge. Another concerns her decision about the dance band and dancing. Where was she to draw the line? She asked the Lord. One night she looked up into the face of a boy with whom she was dancing. "I'm a Christian now," she commented.

"A Christian! What in the world are you doing at a dance?" he blurted.

This, to Val, was the Holy Spirit's answer. A few days later she met the fellows to tell them she was quitting the band. "My life is different now," she told them. "I can't honor the Lord in this way." The fellows figured she would not last. "She'll be back. . . ."

But they were wrong.

Music, however, was still very much a part of her: rhythm within would not be imprisoned. Everywhere she turned she heard jazz, and something inside would respond. So she prayed that the Lord would undertake. And He did! He seemed to lift it out, root and all. The desire for popular music was replaced by a new appreciation of sacred music.

Not many months after her conversion, Val's clear contralto voice became a favorite at youth rallies in the Midwest. At one rally she met a young lady who wanted in on her secret. A Christian and a talented vocalist herself, she was studying for an operatic career. But should she? Val unfolded her own story. Then they prayed and the young lady gave herself completely to the Lord. Operatic ambitions suddenly had taken flight!

In 1947, following graduation from high school, Val felt led to study for the mission field. Someone told her about Prairie Bible Institute, a work-as-you-study school far off the beaten path at Three Hills, Alberta. She applied, then meanwhile, not hearing from Canada, entered a Chicago school; here she was assured of regular singing engagements and could pay her way. But somehow this set-up did not seem to be the Lord's will; Val became strangely restless. Then at the end of her first week a letter came from Canada. She was accepted! But tuition was $165 and train fare almost as much—and Val had only $3.50!

Late Sunday evening she returned to her room after singing for a young people's group in down-state Illinois. She hadn't mentioned her need and naturally her heart skipped when $75 dropped from an envelope the group had given her. Next morning she got $40 from her sister, June, and at the same time a letter arrived from a Christian jeweler, a family friend, enclosing $75 love offering from the church Val attended in Chicago.

And that's why Val ended up as a student at Three Hills, Alberta.

At school she became concerned about Sister June, an occupational therapist at Evanston, Illinois. A Christian since she was 14, June had always been active in young people's work and her spiritual life was strengthened through Inter-Varsity Christian Fellowship at the University of Illinois. But after graduation, her energies were not principally directed toward the things of the Lord, and Val prayed that she might give herself entirely to His will.

In November 1947 June was honestly able to tell the Lord that she was "willing to go anywhere, do anything, regardless of cost, for the glory of the Lord." Val prayed through with her and the way began to unfold. Val's earnest example—plus the missionary emphasis in the Fluegges' home church, and June's searching of the Scriptures and prayer for the Holy Spirit to reveal His will—led her to realize that the Lord would have her to be a missionary for Him. Married now, she and her husband were slated to be in the Philippines by October 1951.

Thus, Valerie Fluegge's story is not entirely her own. For somehow you have to know what has happened to the Fluegge family before you really know Val. And it all began when the blonde in blue jeans dared herself to attend a gospel meeting. That night she made a decision that changed her life. Today, she says: "If there's anything that stands out about my life, it's the reality I've found in Christ."

...he was wrong and admitted it...

10

Life
with Banker Smith

T HE OTHER DAY I chatted an hour
or so with a guest in his room in Chicago's LaSalle Hotel,
then went down to the grill for dinner with him. It did
not surprise me at all when he asked God's blessing on our
meal, or when, following the meal, he left a gospel tract
titled "Take a Tip" after placing his tip under his plate.

This, to me, was the natural thing for him to do. For
in his room I had probed into almost every phase of Harry
R. Smith's life and had uncovered conclusive evidence that he
works hard for: (1) the Lord, seven days a week; and (2)
the Bank of America five and a half days a week.

Among other things, I learned that Harry Smith is one
of the vice presidents of the bank and is in the Corporation
and Bank Relations Department; that the Bank of America
is the world's largest bank, with deposits totaling some
$5,775,000,000, and has 15,000 employees and 525 domestic
branches in California, with foreign branches in London,
Manila, Tokyo, and Shanghai. So powerful is the bank that
one irrational fellow some years ago sought to impress his
hearers by predicting that the Bank of America would turn

out to be the "little horn" of Daniel 7 who will dominate the earth during the Great Tribulation.

Harry Smith, who averages 150 speaking engagements a year for the Lord's cause, has more than once been introduced as "*the* vice president of the Bank of America." He is quick to remind you that there are more than 200 others. "I'm no great shakes of a businessman," he says modestly. "I drive a '48 Dodge and, like any average man, I paid for it on an installment plan." But even so, he seemingly has done pretty well for himself at the Bank of America. He handles accounts in eight states in the Great Lakes area, making semi-annual flying visits to talk big business with scores of large banks and corporations.

When the opportunity arises in conversation with clients, Harry Smith is quick to put in a word for the Lord. For example, some months ago he mentioned that business at a certain Midwestern corporation was extremely good, and was surprised to hear the president respond with, "Yes, the Lord has certainly been good to me."

After further conversation, Smith surmised that the executive was using the expression merely as a figure of speech. Actually he did not have a personal relationship with God. In conversation he told Smith that he had attended Sunday school as a youngster, and figured that, if he lived the best he could, gave the other fellow a square deal, and provided for his family, he was on good terms with God. Tactfully, Smith showed him that he was on the wrong track and proved it by having him read Ephesians 2:8,9, ". . . by grace are ye saved through faith . . . not of works. . . ."

So, being an honest man, the executive admitted he was wrong, and put his trust in Christ as his personal Saviour. That was nearly two years ago and Smith reports his client is going on with the Lord.

Harry Smith, six feet tall and 180 pounds, is athletic looking at 56. He wears rimless glasses, and dresses and looks the part of the hustler-type executive. His hair is graying, but a slight wave in front hints that there's plenty of life beneath the roof. And there is: never at loss for words, he is energetic and quick.

Smith, whose wife, Orpha, died six years ago, lives with his widowed mother in Menlo Park, a San Francisco suburb. A Christian housekeeper sees that his six-room ranch home is kept in order. The banker himself tries his hand at keeping flowers blooming, but admits that a Japanese gardener does most of the work. His son, Malcolm, is studying at the University of California to teach English literature.

A native of Philadelphia, Harry Smith got his first banking job at eighteen with Union Dime Savings Bank of New York. At nineteen he felt the call of the West and for a year worked at the Inter-State Trust Company in Denver. In 1920 he pushed on to Los Angeles and went to work for the Bank of Italy (the name became Bank of America in '31). He was transferred to San Francisco in 1926, and became a vice president in '43. His rise resulted from hard work and study: he was graduated from the Graduate School of Banking of Rutgers University in 1937. He studied so hard in the American Institute of Banking, largest adult education movement in the world, that he was named to head it in 1939-40.

Smith can recite stories of incidents which occurred during AIB and other banking conventions to show how he handles the highball, No. 1 drink for most business conventions.

"What's yours?" the waiter will ask.

"Make mine a Coke," Smith will say in a matter-of-fact tone.

"What do you want in it?" the waiter asks automatically.

"Ice—and nothing else."

More often than not, Smith says, someone else will order the same, and later amble up and confess, "You know, Harry,

I wanted Coke all the time, but didn't have nerve enough to ask for it."

Smith never did drink, but he used to pay out plenty for smokes. In a backslidden condition in the middle '30s, he burned up about a package of cigarettes a day. However, the Lord solved that, but quick.

At a meeting held by the Christian Business Men's Committee he heard Bishop J. Taylor Smith say: "If there's anything in your life on which you can't ask the Lord's blessing, the sooner you get rid of it the better."

"That was the end of smoking for me," Harry Smith says.

Seemingly, Banker Smith has always been quick to admit it when he was wrong. For instance, when he was a boy he had an idea that a recording angel jotted down his good and bad deeds, and at the end of time God would look at the record. If the good out-balanced the bad, God would give him a harp and wings and send him to join the heavenly choir. However, when he was twenty, Smith got the right slant on how God really works things.

Under the preaching of famed Dr. R. A. Torrey in the Church of the Open Door in Los Angeles, he realized that he could not possibly save himself, that "good" never cancels out the "bad" in God's plan. Christ, he found, was the only solution to the sin question. So, he did the logical thing: he received Christ as his personal Saviour. This meant that he had quit trying to work his way into heaven and was trusting Christ instead.

Later, Harry Smith learned something else new. Besides purchasing his salvation, Christ also had purchased the man Harry Smith. So, in a Christian Endeavor convention two years after he was saved, he yielded completely to the Lord. "In California," Smith goes on to illustrate what happened, "some people sell property, reserving mineral rights. This means that if oil, for instance, is found on the property the original owner can return and take over part or all of the profits. The Lord wants Christians without reservations, and that's the transaction I made at the Christian Endeavor meeting."

This important decision has paid off for Harry Smith. That is why both at home and away, he is constantly on the job for the Lord. One of his favorite home projects is the Peninsula Bible Fellowship in nearby suburban Palo Alto, a community church organized by Smith and several other Christian men. They carry the work on each Sunday, and meet early on Tuesday mornings for prayer before driving into San Francisco for work.

Another keen interest is in the Christian Business Men's Committee movement. This fellowship, Smith says, has been a great spiritual blessing through contact with other business-men of like faith and desire to make the Saviour known. He was chairman of the San Francisco committee for two years and later vice chairman of the International Committee.

So, doing two full-time jobs at once, for the Lord and the Bank of America, Vice President Harry Smith is doubly busy. Yet he manages to do both jobs well and enjoys life. When I left him following our visit at the hotel he was heading for his room. It was about 7:30 and he would dictate to a Sound-Scriber for an hour or so to cover his day's business, check over his books, and then spend time with the Lord. His hobby is collecting books and that day he had picked up a rare 1911 translation of the Bible. That night I knew at least one banker would close the day reading from the Book that has given him the answer to life here and hereafter.

...the decision wasn't easy...

11

I am a Life-Termer

as told by John Robertson, and written
in collaboration with the author

JUST FOR THE RECORDS I might mention that I'm 24. I was born on April 8, 1927, in the middle of a west Texas sandstorm in Sweetwater. Most fellows in their early twenties are either in school or starting careers of some sort. Many have already married and are starting homes of their own. But not me. I'm in prison. Huntsville prison, near Houston, Texas, is my home for life.

I'm not kicking, understand. These are just the facts. When you kill a man, there's a penalty to pay. And I'm paying it. Yet at the same time, I'm serving the Lord.

Before we go into that, however, perhaps you'd better hear my story from the beginning:

My parents separated when I was only six years of age. I remember my father fairly well. He was a cook. After their separation I lived with my grandmother for several years until Mother remarried and I went to live with her in Houston where my home has been ever since.

Following graduation from Jeff Davis High, I enlisted in the Navy and served two years. Shortly after my discharge in July 1946 I went to work and in the year that followed I held six different jobs, as a truck driver and salesman. I wasn't satisfied with any of them and continued to grow restless and more dissatisfied.

So one Saturday—July 12, 1947—I was ready for almost anything. I was angry for I had just changed jobs the week before and already I wanted to change again. In this sort of mood I met two buddies whom we'll call Ron and Dick, and we set out to make a day of it.

About the middle of the afternoon I suggested that we hold up and rob a liquor store on Humble Road, near Houston. At first we joked about it, then I did a super-salesmanship on Ron and Dick. Neither of them wanted to be hijackers. Still, I'd passed by the liquor store several times and thought what an easy place it would be to hold up and make a getaway.

Don't ask me why I ever thought it. I didn't read comic books and crime magazines. I liked listening to classical music and being with my friends better than anything else. But I got this crazy idea.

At 5 o'clock I got an old Luger 7.65 from my room along with some old clothes I was going to wear. Since it was too early to start anything we cruised about in the car. Shortly before 9 o'clock we drove by the store three times to make sure the way was clear, then pulled off on a side road to change to old clothes. It was out of town about five miles and there were very few houses. There were no cars on the highway when we stopped in front of the store long enough for Dick and me to get out; then Ron drove out of the light and parked heading toward town with the lights off and motor running.

We entered the store and walked up to the counter. I was about half a step behind my buddy. There were two people there, a man and a woman, both of which I judged to be in their middle fifties. The man looked at me as if he knew what was going to happen. I asked if he had any wine in stock, and he seemed to stall. Fearing to delay any longer, I drew my Luger, which I had in my belt under the green field-jacket I was wearing. He jumped, and I told him that he knew what I wanted and to hand it over. He was angry but reached under the counter to get a cigar box which I guessed had the money in it. He held it out to Dick but started to wave it back and forth. My buddy grabbed it, but the man held on. Then as I started to help take the box from him he reached for his hip pocket. I heard a shot fired and saw him let go of the money and fall. I realized that I had killed him. We fled with the money and jumped into the car and headed for Houston. When we reached Houston we separated and did not meet again.

The following Monday morning I re-enlisted in the Navy, but found I had blood poisoning in my right arm; so for a week while the police were running down clues I was in the naval hospital in Houston. After my release I went to San Diego for duty.

More than a year passed. During that time I led an uneasy and watchful life, although I didn't believe that the authorities would ever get me. But I was still on edge. All of it, however, wasn't due to the trouble that I was in; rather I was seeking again the same thing which I had thought that robbery might provide: *excitement,* which had cost an innocent man his life. Still I couldn't find anything that brought lasting pleasure.

One afternoon in July I went to San Diego on liberty. It was Saturday and a buddy and I wanted to go to a movie since there wasn't much else to do to kill time. As we walked up Broadway a fellow of about my own age handed us a card and invited us to the Youth for Christ meeting which was being held that evening at the First Baptist Church. We told him "some other time" and crossed the street to the movie.

At the movie I suddenly felt that I wanted to go to that meeting. My buddy wouldn't hear of it so I left him and headed on up the street to the church. I had been taught as a child to go to church and had joined the church when I was about 12, but did not understand what it was all about. I stopped going to church before I was out of high school.

They were singing when I arrived and the speaker had not yet been introduced. An usher gave me a program and found me a seat and I began to sing with the rest. The speaker, I found, was a fellow Texan, Clifton Brannon.

He caught and held my interest from the very start. Gradually I noticed I was sweating and felt as if every word he spoke was for me alone. I didn't know it at the time but I was under conviction by the Holy Spirit. When the invitation was given I went forward and accepted the Lord Jesus Christ as my own personal Saviour and knew that salvation was mine.

Just what Mr. Brannon said I'm not sure, but I do know that the power of God was there and convicted me of my sinful condition, and of my need for a Saviour from sin, and I accepted Him.

This was a Saturday night in July, and right after this I left San Diego on board my ship, the U.S.S. *Chilton,* a PA 38. The ship took me to San Francisco where I was on duty for three weeks, then I got orders back to San Diego.

I knew I was a born-again Christian, but still I was not leading a victorious Christian life. One of the Youth for Christ workers invited me to a mountain Bible camp for an evening meeting. George Cowan, a missionary to Mexico, spoke, and I felt moved to talk to him after the service. I told him I was seeking the will of God in my life and asked him questions about the mission fields and work. We prayed for a revelation of our Father's will to me concerning my life.

I had come up to the mountain camp in the youth worker's car but, as he was staying the next day, I arranged to return to San Diego with another sailor by the name of Rusty. About four the next morning the two of us got up and headed back to the base. It was nearly an hour's trip and as we started down the mountains I felt an urge to tell Rusty about the trouble I had gotten into in Houston. At first I wouldn't give in to such a notion but finally did and told him the whole story.

Rusty didn't say that I should go back or stay, but asked instead if I had ever thought that perhaps it might be the will of God that I go back. We parted on that trend of thought, me refusing to even consider going back, and Rusty not saying much. He knew that I was fighting it out in myself.

Back at the base I had to face the question. Was it the will of God that I return and stand trial? Since I had asked for Him to reveal His will to me, might I not be rejecting His revelation by refusing to consider this? I stood convicted; I had refused to even consider going back, and now within myself I prayed, knowing the answer, "Lord, Thy will be done."

That night after all others had turned in, I had a long talk with a dear brother in Christ, Will Bruce, the San Diego YFC director. We discussed my decision and the time ahead of me.

It was decided that it would be better to get a leave from the Navy and turn myself over to the Houston authorities. My commanding officer gave me leave about a week later, and I started home.

Several rides took me as far as Gila Bend where I

arrived at about 8 o'clock at night. After a bite to eat I walked out on the highway to catch another ride. Within a few minutes a truck pulled up to the cafe and the driver went inside to eat. Walking over to the truck I noticed that it was out of Dallas, and that was just what I wanted. Dallas was only 200 miles from home and the truck would make good time. I went inside the cafe and I asked the driver for a ride. He told me to go ahead and climb in. The truck had a sleeper on it and in about an hour I crawled into it and went to sleep.

The next morning our conversation turned to Christ. The driver seemed interested, so I gave him my own testimony, going on to tell him how Christ was for him as well. About 50 miles from El Paso he surrendered to the Saviour. He tossed his cigarettes out of the window and did not smoke again the rest of the time I was with him.

My last ride took me right to my own doorstep, and I was home after hitchhiking 1,700 miles. My parents never knew until the day I surrendered what had happened. My testimony was used to lead two of my buddies to my Lord before I turned in.

On September 7 I talked to a prominent Baptist minister, and through a friend he arranged for me to surrender to the District Attorney. The next day at 2 o'clock, in company with this same minister, I surrendered.

I was in jail for almost five months awaiting trial. Some of the prisoners said I would be sorry; others said I was a fanatic, and several said I was right. While I awaited trial the Holy Spirit used me to lead 15 men to the Lord. One of these, a boy of about 20, was hard to reach. He admitted he was a sinner and eternally lost without Christ, but would go no farther. I prayed for a chance to speak to him again and then one night I got that chance. He was reading the Bible and after a few minutes of conversation he accepted the Saviour with tears in his eyes.

On January 17 my trial came off. It was short. My confession was read and the District Attorney said a few words. The jury then debated for about five minutes and returned a verdict of guilty and life imprisonment.

Huntsville—my home today—reminds me in a way of a naval base. There is about the same sort of discipline, and about the same relation between the officials and the men.

There is every opportunity to witness to men and lead them to Christ. I have an hour free-time on the yard each weekday, half a day Saturday, and all day Sunday. I let each man set the pattern of Scripture and appeal that I use on him. About the only thing that I always do is to depend fully upon the Holy Spirit for soul-winning power. I use different verses for different men. For instance, if a man tells me how he has had no friend nor loved one to write him or care for him, then I tell him first of his sin, then of One who would be his Friend and who would care for him. Others need the solemn warnings of eternal damnation to convict their hearts of their need.

As I write this, I can count 23 men who have accepted the Lord since I came here. God has also led me to take a Bible correspondence course, and I am vice-president and assistant teacher of our Prisoners' Christian Association, which boasts about 100 members. We have a Bible class to bring new Christians into fellowship with one another and try to get them to reading the Word, letting the one Teacher, the Holy Spirit, interpret to them the true meaning.

My plans for my stay here in prison are set on one course—the will of my Lord. One thing is sure: whatever the job, it will be primarily for the purpose of using me to bring souls to the Saviour.

If the Lord should see fit to sometime have me pardoned, again I can only say that my life would be governed by His will, no matter what.

...he called a stockholders' meeting...

12

Selling Florida
is His Business

Some years ago the Florida Motor Lines wanted a modern bus terminal in Miami. Looking about for a good location, executives soon turned to Kenneth S. Keyes, president of The Keyes Company, Realtors, who convinced them that the logical site was N.E. Street at Third Avenue.

The property owner was approached and he agreed to erect the building for investment purposes. Plans were drawn and approved, the lease was drafted and okayed by attorneys for both sides. With the deal nearly closed Keyes felt pretty good: an $1,800 commission wasn't bad! But two days before final papers were to be signed, Keyes got bad news. The owner, without warning, had backed out; he wouldn't build after all. And no amount of reasoning could budge him!

Finally, the owner agreed to lease the land and let Keyes himself erect the structure if he could finance it—and it was a big "if" in those days when everything in Miami was at low ebb. However, the real-estate executive hurdled the "if," erecting the building with bus company funds—unusual since the bus people had previously refused to build for themselves!

91

As a result of the sudden change in plans, Keyes netted almost as much each year for a decade as the original commission of $1,800. In other words, it was nearly ten times more profitable than the original deal, which had been so strangely blocked!

"You can call me superstitious if you want to," says Ken Keyes, whose real-estate firm ranks as Florida's largest, "but I'm just old-fashioned enough to believe that this illustrates how God will bless the person who makes Him his silent Partner in life and business."

And that is just what Keyes, a stocky, magnetic, go-getting sort of fellow, has done. After tithing his personal income for several years, he called his stockholders together in 1938 and announced his plans to make God a silent Partner in his growing business. This bylaw was duly seconded and passed:

"We, the stockholders of The Keyes Company, recognizing God's ownership of all things we possess, and realizing that we are but His stewards here on earth, wish to acknowledge His ownership and our stewardship, and to that end it is hereby resolved that we adopt God's plan of using one-tenth of our profits for church and charitable purposes."

This plan, Keyes believes, is a big reason why the company's books for 1950 show a $16 million business volume. Tithes from the profits go to churches "that preach the old fundamental doctrines in contrast to the new, modernistic doctrines," and to charity groups. The fund supports a missionary in Korea.

Ken Keyes (whose name rhymes with "skies") did not start tithing until he entered the real-estate field—although he had been a born-again Christian a number of years since school days in Michigan. He went south during World War I and decided to stay in Atlanta, Georgia. Here, after entering the advertising business, Keyes became deeply interested in God's Word. Having accepted a Sunday-school class of boys nearly as old as himself, he "had to dig deep into the Bible to keep ahead of them."

During the boom of the '20s, Keyes visited Miami and decided to get into real-estate business for himself. Leaving his boys' class and thriving advertising business, he landed in an atmosphere where newsboys rolled dice for $100 bills and real estate changed hands many times a day to the tune of millions of dollars—on paper.

Then came the crash of '29. "Things blew right up in our faces," Keyes recalls. So as a result, he was forced to start his business during the Great Depression—from scratch! And, oddly enough, in 1932, when going was toughest, Keyes put God's tithing program into action. Until then, God was given the leftovers. Now He was to get His share first. Giving a tenth of everything was hard, to be sure— for the income itself was barely enough for family needs. But before long the nine-tenths was more than the whole income had been.

The following year Keyes' income was up 60 per cent; the second year, 100 per cent. And by the third year it was more than three times the original. "Everything we did seemed to prosper," Keyes says. "And the more we gave to God's work, the more money He entrusted to us. Today our tithe is more than our entire income was in 1932."

The Keyes Company occupies offices in the Keyes Building on busy Biscayne Boulevard in Miami, and is the scene each Monday morning of a 15-minute devotional service for employees. The International News Service, preparing a feature on devotional services in business and industrial firms, sent a young newsman to get the inside story on The Keyes Company service. And it proved to be a visit that the newsman will never forget. For in Keyes' office, with its modern-as-tomorrow equipment and a big tropical plant in the corner, the visitor revealed to Keyes that he was not a real Christian. President Keyes then brought the subject around to a personal relationship with God, and they wound up on their knees with the newsman pouring out his heart to God in acceptance of Jesus as Saviour.

Inside the main office of The Keyes Company are formidable rows of desks and at each a specialist in some phase of real estate. Each salesman makes it a point to back up the company slogan: "A Firm that Makes and Keeps Friends." From Keyes on down, they are a business-like bunch. "Nowhere in the Bible," maintains Keyes, "do we find that God frowns on money or making money. In Paul's letter to Timothy, the Scriptures say plainly that *'the love* of money is the root of all evil.'* He did not blame money as such."

The Keyes Company, incidentally, is only one of Keyes' business enterprises. He is chairman of the board of Keyes-Ozen Insurance Agency, one of Miami's largest insurance firms; is president of the corporation which owns the 520-room Everglades Hotel on Miami's bayfront; and president also of Rainbow Springs Enterprises, operating Rainbow Springs, the famous resort and attraction on U.S. 41, near Dunnellon, Florida; owns a 120-acre Persian lime and avocado grove, and recently acquired sole ownership of Radio Station WMBM, which he is using to promote his enterprises and to give a real Christian testimony to the south Florida area.

Despite his many business interests, Ken Keyes accepts invitations from churches from coast to coast to speak as a layman, about the Lord's money. When transportation difficulties threatened his ministry some years ago, he bought a fast cabin plane, made one of his assistants—an AAF vet— his pilot. He delivers his message "In Partnership With God" about forty times a year. Once he delivered it thirteen times in four days! The message in booklet form has had a nation-wide circulation of more than a million copies. His Miami office will supply copies, without cost, in any reasonable quantity.

Keyes turns thumbs down when pay is mentioned for the ministry. He even pays his own traveling expenses. Only once, he recalls, did he accept—and then six months in advance. His "fee": a savory Virginia ham for a series of stewardship talks.

A typical example of those who heed to Keyes' advice to follow in God's tithing plan is one of his own ex-salesmen. In 1935 he was $500 in debt. He started tithing. In 1936 he paid off the loan before it was due and had $1200 in cash, with which he opened his own real-estate business. In 1937 he earned $7890; in 1938, $10,843; in 1939, $15,143; and in 1940, $17,499.

Deeply interested in Sunday-school work since he taught his boys' class in Atlanta, Kenneth S. Keyes has served two separate terms of three years each as Sunday-school superintendent of Shenandoah Presbyterian Church, Miami, where he is an elder. But on Sundays and weekdays, his advice to young Christians remains the same: "Recognize early in life that all you have—time, energy, abilities, and money—is a trust from God; then resolve to be good stewards of these gifts. If you do not feel led into full-time Christian work, use a liberal portion of your time, energy, abilities and money for Him."

...he stopped under a big tree...

13

This is
Pedro's Garage

I n May 1950 I visited Niagara Falls for the first time. On the way up from Buffalo we took a side trip to Ransomville, N. Y., a quiet little town of about 1,000 population. There I ran across something more fascinating to me than mighty Niagara, as spectacular as it is with its endless rush of churning waters.

It is Pedro's Garage.

Now, garages do not usually interest me—except when I have car trouble. But fortunately someone previously had tipped me off to Pedro's. The building itself is not unusual, though nice enough. It is a neat concrete block structure, housing the garage and a display room for Willys automobiles. Next door is a used-car lot and out front is a neon sign: "Pedro's Garage."

Like at Niagara eighteen miles to the west, you'll also find an awsome flood of power at work at Pedro's. Only here the power is quiet and you are not readily conscious of it. You must talk to the workers and snoop about. Only then do you get something of an idea that Pedro's is much more than an ordinary garage, with its grease monkeys and hydraulic jacks and oil-stained floors. Here is a unique center of evangelism and headquarters for a thriving missionary work nearly 3,000 miles away in Puerto Rico.

Unfortunately, Pedro Ortiz, the 48-year-old little Puerto Rican who operates the business—along with a car agency in Lockport, N. Y. — was not around. He was in Buffalo for an important dealers' meeting. But I learned the inside story from Duane Reese, then Pedro's shop manager, a born-again Christian who conducts a weekly gospel mission service in a poor section of Niagara Falls.

Reese, who since has resigned to operate a flower business, showed me the ledger in the bookkeeper's office. It was like any other ledger, with names and addresses and debits and credits. But to the gang at Pedro's it means much more. Each name represents a soul for whom Christ died. Special invitations are mailed monthly to all of Pedro's customers, inviting them to attend a Friday night evangelistic service. The man who got his carburetor fixed up last month may come in this month and in the same barn-like garage have his sin-sick soul made new in an encounter with Christ. For here on meeting night hospitalized autos are rolled out back, garage equipment is pushed aside, and the oil-stained floor is scrubbed in preparation for a full-fledged gospel service. Chairs are set up and a piano—a fixture in Pedro's display room—is rolled in. All of which helps only slightly to make the place look like a church.

But customers and their families from miles around—many of whom would be reluctant to attend church—feel at home in the unique setting and the friendly atmosphere. Attendance averages upwards of 100. The gospel is preached in all its fullness, by visiting speakers or by Pedro himself. Hardly a monthly service passes without decisions for Christ. The week before I visited Pedro's, a family of three found salvation through Christ: Dad and Mother and their 13-year-old daughter who was then a budding rodeo star. One man, drunk most of the time, sobered up long enough to purchase a used car from Pedro. An invitation to one of the monthly services, plus his wife's prayers, brought him under the sound of the gospel. Today he's an out-and-out Christian. Bob, then a 29-year-old mechanic at Pedro's, was among those saved at a meeting in early 1950. He had been employed at the garage for about two months.

From time to time, as the Holy Spirit leads, Pedro or one of the gang will give a customer a man-to-man talk about the gospel. Some storm out mad, other go away glad. If customers are around at 2 P.M.—the hour for the daily prayer meeting at Pedro's garage—they are invited to join the gang in prayer. One man wanted to be excused because he had prayed just that morning—but they gently urged and he came anyhow. Some stammer that they do not know how to pray—but they learn.

I missed seeing Pedro Ortiz, as I have mentioned, but all 130 pounds of this dark, little man undoubtedly are dedicated wholly to the Lord. The story behind Pedro is unusual in itself. Far from being a Christian when he came to the States from Puerto Rico in 1926 to work, he came under strong gospel preaching in a Methodist church in 1936, and was convicted of sin and his need of Christ as Saviour. One day while driving from Ransomville to Niagara Falls he stopped under a big tree and prayed it out. He turned his back on sin and let the blood of Christ do the cleansing.

With Christ in his heart, old habits dropped off. He lost his desire for strong drink. His music (he plays the saxophone) changed from jazz to old hymns and gospel songs. One day also, he threw away his pipe, after hearing a message on the indwelling presence of the Holy Spirit in the heart of the believer. After all, he was a temple of the Holy Spirit—and tobacco only smoked up the temple.

Today Puerto Rico is still extremely close to Pedro's heart. Pedro's Garage in Ransomville is U. S. headquarters for a Puerto Rican mission program that sponsors seven churches and salaried pastors. Pedro's oldest brother, Maximo, resigned a government position to supervise the work and to pastor one of the churches. The seven churches were built one by one, springing up as the people of one church won their neighbors to Christ. Churches are situated on or nearby the military highway which encircles the island. Pedro's mother is listed among the many converts.

Pedro himself, with the aid of his brothers and native workers, in 1940 preached to his people for a month, then left the work in the hands of the workers. He returned again in 1941 to hold another evangelistic campaign, and helped erect the "mother church."

Natives from a radius of eight miles walked to the gospel services, despite malicious opposition from certain religious leaders who rule most of the native population. One native came to put an end to the meetings. He stood outside an open window, a dagger concealed in his shirt. When Pedro mounted the platform, the native planned to hurl the dagger and end the "fanatical" preaching. But before Pedro arose to preach, a storm blew up from nowhere and the shutters were quickly closed, foiling the plot. The incident was revealed when the would-be assassin was converted in a revival that later broke out.

I might have easily overlooked one interesting angle of the Puerto Rican mission work had it not been for a can of oil I picked up in Pedro's office. It was labeled "Modern Motor Oil," but the distributor's name caught my eye: "Ortiz Bros." This brand of oil, I was told, is shipped from a refinery in Ohio to Puerto Rico and the bulk of the profits helps finance the gospel work. Pedro's two brothers and five sisters, all 100 per cent behind the program, conduct the oil business on the island.

And, from all indications, business must be booming in Puerto Rico. Back in Ransomville, for instance, Pedro's garage was up against it temporarily. A bill for $10,000 had to be paid in a matter of hours. Pedro managed to scrape up $9,000. But where could they get another thousand? The gang prayed about it and left the problem with the Lord. The answer came from Puerto Rico: a check for $1000 from oil profits, a complete surprise to the gang at Ransomville!

The fact that they were short of cash does not mean that business is poor at Pedro's. Thousands of dollars flow through the business almost daily. Business is good enough in Ransomville, in fact, to keep three busy in the shop and two working in the office, besides supplying after-school work for three of Pedro's sons. Even Mrs. Pedro (as friends call his wife) frequently comes around to help.

Pedro himself often works until after midnight and the gang does not see him until 10 or 10:30 next morning. He would be there earlier, except for the fact that he spends an hour and a half alone with the Lord after arising.

This practice makes it easy for him to live close to the Lord at the garage. Here is a portion of a prayer that I found typed on a "Pedro Motors" letterhead hanging beside his desk:

". . . I give Thee my credit and reputation: may I never value it, but only in respect of Thee: nor endeavor to maintain it, but as it may do Thee service and advance Thy honor in the world . . ."

This, I concluded, is really the secret of Pedro's Garage. The things you see—new cars, oil cans, automobile parts, and greasy tools—are not unusual. It's what you can't see— the Power of God quietly working there and in far-away Puerto Rico—that makes Pedro's more unforgettable than roaring Niagara!

...the department was swamped...

14

Bristol's Help
Department and President Smith

O<small>NE NIGHT IN THE</small> late spring of 1947
a man from Bristol, R. I., William H. Smith by name, tossed
in his Pullman berth as his train rumbled northward through
the darkness somewhere in the Southland. It was hot and
sticky and a group of college kids going home for vacation
were celebrating. So, unable to sleep, Smith began to muse.
Treasurer of Bristol Manufacturing Corporation, makers of
fabric and waterproof footwear, he was thinking about
business: "What are we doing in our organization that is
absolutely unselfish?"

It was a penetrating question. A Christian since childhood, Bill Smith believed that the Christian life should be
an unselfish one and figured that any business founded on
Christian principles should also in some way reflect unselfishness. Everything he could think of at Bristol Manufacturing
was for gain. The shoes, certainly, were sold for profit. Pen-
sions and a public relations department were in a sense re-
flecting unselfishness already, but all gave returns in the
long run.

103

Suddenly this thought occurred to him: why not get a minister, give him an office and a secretary, and tell him to take orders directly from the Lord—not from company executives or anyone else?

Later, back at the plant, he tried to sell his brother, Bristol President Maurice, on the idea. Though a Christian since he was 18, Maurice thought it was a crackpot idea, that it would not work in business. But he prayed about it and they laid plans for a Department of Christian Relations. Maurice talked their idea over with the Rev. Dale D. Dutton, pastor of Central Baptist Church, Providence, and he liked it so well that he resigned his church and became vice-president in charge of the new department.

Although originally given a parish within a 25-mile radius of Bristol, Dr. Dutton soon was shuttling back and forth across the nation when newspapers and magazines gave the plan world-wide publicity. His job: *do good*. Today he continues this. On Monday he may help a widow in Dallas obtain work in order to feed her starving children, and on Tuesday counsel a man at the point of deserting his wife and children.

Almost from the start Dr. Dutton has been so swamped with requests for help that President Maurice pitches in and for the most part lets the other executives and its 800 employees manufacture the rubber shoes. As a result, today Smith, a ruddy-faced, ruggedly built man who looks and dresses like a college football coach, devotes nearly all of his working time to the Department of Christian Relations. He personally answers many of the hundreds of letters that pour in from the four corners of the earth, interviews troubled persons and fills speaking engagements over the country. With Dr. Dutton and brother Bill, Maurice Smith has found the Department of Christian Relations a real road paved for soul-winning. Knowing the Lord Jesus Christ as personal

Saviour is the answer to all problems, the Smith brothers believe.

An aged man needs a pair of shoes. An elderly woman needs cash for an operation on her eyes. A convict needs a typewriter to help him write to earn money for the family at home. All get guidance and advice and deserving cases get material assistance. But all comers, honest and dishonest alike, are advised to look to Christ.

President Smith says that they have received upwards of 100,000 letters since 1947, and, although only God keeps the records, he estimates conversions would run into the thousands. "Even if we were privileged to help only one soul to find his way to heaven we would consider our efforts well worthwhile."

One interesting story that started with a problem and ended in salvation concerns two businessmen. Owners of a gift shop, they were not making a go of it. Maybe the Smiths could come up with a solution. So, Maurice Smith analyzed their problems and suggested, among other things, that they reduce buying. He ended his letter by pointing out their need of Jesus Christ. Later, as business improved, Smith sent a Christian businessman in the same town to help further, and after two or three visits he led one of the men to Christ. The other, however, could not quit his sins and prayer began to go up in Bristol, nearly a thousand miles away.

Soon after Palm Sunday the following year, Smith received a letter from his Christian contact man. The businessman for whom they had been praying had called regarding another human problem, this had been solved, and once again Christ had been suggested as the eternal solution. Result: the man finally recognized himself as a lost sinner and walked to the altar on Palm Sunday morning to publicly confess Christ as personal Saviour. Today the two business associates, brothers in Christ, conduct a daily devotional service at their business.

The Smiths do not pretend to do their job alone. Much credit, they readily point out, goes to the Christian "field men" who make many of the personal contacts. Briefly, here is how the machinery operates: a letter comes for help; a reply is sent; a carbon copy of the reply goes to a "field man" and he follows up the problem. The contact man may be a pastor, a Christian salesman, a Gideon, or perhaps a member of a local Christian Business Men's Committee.

In California not long ago a Gideon hopped into his car at Maurice Smith's signal and hurried to see a Jew who had written Bristol regarding a human problem. Much correspondence regarding the problem passed between Bristol and California and finally the Jew wrote to thank Smith for sending the man to visit him, saying that he had taken him through the Old Testament and had not even mentioned Christ. However, when he got to the New Testament he showed him that the prophecy had been fulfilled concerning the Messiah and that Christ, after all, was his Messiah. It resulted in the Jew receiving Christ as Saviour.

Two years before, the Californian confided, a man had tried to win him but had used an approach that closed him up like a clam: "Accept Christ or you'll go to hell!" The statement was 100 per cent true, but the approach proved bad. Smith adds this thought: "We'd go broke in business if we used such poor methods as we often do in soul-winning."

Thus, the Department of Christian Relations operates differently from the average soul-winning group. To the Bristol people, soul-winning is a selling job and they never give up after merely one try. Maurice Smith puts it this way: "Suppose a St. Louis store wrote us saying that the store was interested in handling Bristolite products. Immediately machinery would begin to move: a sales correspondent would check to see if the store's account was good, and, if so, a letter would be written selling them further on Bristolite products, and advising them that a salesman would call shortly. Perhaps the store would not be sold the first time and the salesman would have to return again and again until he had the purchasing agent's name on the dotted line. There's a thrill to such because there's opposition."

And so it is, Smith points out, that the Christian relations department works. A letter comes asking for advice on a human problem and, with the Holy Spirit's guidance, no stone is left unturned as efforts are made to acquaint the troubled individual with the solver of all problems, the Lord Jesus Christ. Smith recalls one case which was closed only after 140 pages of correspondence had been written. The person involved was an ex-GI who, after discharge, went on a crime spree. He left a trail of petty crimes and finally landed in jail after passing a worthless check. He got ten years, with a flock of detainers against him. He wrote the Bristol Corporation for help and a Christian businessman called on him and won him to Christ. At liberty following his prison release and after receiving a deferred sentence in Rhode Island, he is today a virtual ward of Smith and is working at Bristol Manufacturing and studying for full-time Christian service.

The Bristol Manufacturing Corporation had a lot of critics when the Department of Christian Relations was launched. Some customers decided to buy elsewhere, among them a large department store that did thousands of dollars worth of business with Bristol. The outlook was dark. Lost business the first year ran to something like $650,000, and the $491,000 income tax refund failed to cover. However, as the months rolled by, the company gained new friends and the large account came back with even bigger orders. So business has actually been helped by the addition of the unique department—and that was not the original purpose of the department. To illustrate further, in one year shortly after the dark period, a year when the industry as a whole dipped 20 per cent in sales, due to a mild winter in most sections (boots and other waterproof footwear naturally sell best in nasty weather), Bristol showed an increase of 15 per cent.

Could this increased business volume have any connection with the words of Christ: "If any man serve me, him will my Father honor" (John 12:26)? Maurice Smith thinks so.

Yet it is not the increased business volume that gives President Maurice Smith the most satisfaction. Naturally, increased sales are nice (the Bristol people are not in business for their health), but he is happiest when he is helping a lost sinner find Christ as personal Saviour.

His hardest and most unusual case?

Take the case of the professor of English in a large University in India. He belonged to a sect of fire worshipers and wrote Smith regarding a problem after reading about the Christian Relations venture in *The Reader's Digest*. After his reply, Smith wrote a Christian worker in India who promptly reported that the man was hopeless, being part of a group that could never be reached with the gospel.

But Smith is not licked that easily. Beginning in April 1949, he wrote letter after letter explaining the gospel, showing the necessity of receiving Christ into the heart. He pointed out clearly that "all have sinned" and that Christ, God in human flesh, took upon Himself on Calvary's cross the sins of every human being. His resurrection, Smith showed further, guarantees eternal life to the repentant sinner who personally receives the risen Christ.

Finally, Smith's efforts were rewarded. In June 1950— more than a year after the correspondence began!—another letter arrived from India, this time signed, "Yours in Christ." In September 1951 Smith met the ex-fire worshiper in New York City and later personally enrolled him in a Christian school where he is studying for his Ph.D. degree.

So it is no wonder that Maurice Smith and his brother Bill, along with other folks at Bristol Manufacturing Corporation, think it worthwhile to take time off from making footwear and other items. They are helping people find the only solution to this life . . . and the one to come!

...he heard himself sing...

15

What Happened
to the Singing Man

W ITH THE SUN RISING back of the rugged California hills that Easter morning in 1950 at famed Hollywood Bowl in Los Angeles, mustached Persian tenor Lutar Hoobyar stepped to the microphone to sing an all-time favorite, "The Old Rugged Cross." A thrill shot through the audience as his strong, clear voice rang out in the natural bowl beneath a cloudless sky. Even among the hundreds of thousands listening on radios across the nation and over the world goose-flesh crawled as Hoobyar's singing made the rugged cross seem so *real*, so *important*.

Here and there someone flicked a tear from his eye as Hoobyar finished, "I'll cherish the old rugged cross . . . And exchange it some day for a crown." As the handsome tenor returned to his place on the platform, he knew his song had been a success.

But success was nothing new to Lutar Hoobyar. Behind him were 25 years of opera, concert, and motion pictures. This was just another appearance—though he had accepted it gladly at the invitation of a friend.

Following the sunrise service, the Mutual Broadcasting

111

Company gave Hoobyar a tape recording of the Hollywood Bowl program. Perhaps he would like to hear himself sing. Maybe he would like again to hear ex-Hollywood starlet Colleen Townsend tell the story of the first Easter.

Lutar Hoobyar did not know it—but this tape recording would be used in changing the entire course of his life! Not that he particularly wanted his life changed, but a miracle was to take place.

Later, about midnight, the dark, handsome tenor sat alone in his living room in Manhattan Beach, Calif., his wife, Mary, and two sons, Tommy, ten, and Peter, six, asleep elsewhere in the house. The sunrise service was taking place all over again—with the aid of Mutual's tape recording. Somehow he had missed a lot that morning—Colleen Townsend's Easter story this time took him back to that empty tomb. And then that strong, clear tenor—and the words of the song:

> ". . . In the old rugged cross,
>   Stained with blood so divine,
> A wondrous beauty I see;
>   For 'twas on that old cross
> Jesus suffered and died,
>   To pardon and sanctify me . . ."*

Tears smarted in his eyes: ". . . to *pardon* and *sanctify me* . . ."

The words still pounding in his ears, Hoobyar fell to his knees beside the tape recorder. He could almost see Jesus hanging on the cross . . . it seemed that the Lord beckoned for him to look up. Now trembling like a leaf, Hoobyar looked and prayed that He would forgive his sins and asked Him to save him for life and eternity. Then and there he opened his heart to the Saviour.

This was not a man experiencing a mental breakdown, nor was he giving way to sentimentalism. Rather for the

---

* Copyright 1913, Renewal 1941, the Rodeheaver Company, owner.

112

first time in his life, Lutar Hoobyar was facing stark reality—facing the Saviour for complete forgiveness of sin, and acknowledging his need for God to control his life!

He says: "That night I immediately felt free of every sinful fetter that had come into my life. The Lord took out all evil desires and replaced them with new desires."

Today he no longer sings for applause; instead, his one aim is to sing and preach the glorious gospel into the hearts of people the country over. Soon after his conversion while singing for Evangelist Merv Rosell in Long Beach, Hoobyar was moved to dedicate his talents to full-time gospel service.

Hoobyar, who now goes by Luther instead of Lutar (Persian for Luther), believes with his heart that since Christ changed him He can change any life. During his long and varied musical career, he caroused from Paris (he studied in Europe, three years) to New York and on to Hollywood, where he played in films during the '30s. Certain revelings in dens of sin along the Seine in Paris could not be described in these pages. He sums it up this way: "I led such a horrible, sinful life that I broke all of God's ten commandments."

Born in Persia, where his parents were converted from Mohammedanism to Christ by zealous Presbyterian missionaries, Luther Hoobyar got a jolt when he came to the United States as a youngster.

Dad Hoobyar, swallowing a story in Chicago about a dream estate for his sons in California with flower gardens and windmills, shelled out. When the family got to California, they found he had bought just another piece of sandy desert, with California poppies, butterflies, jack rabbits, lizards, snakes, and coyotes. Later a horse trader sold the Hoobyars a horse — and once again they found they had been duped. The horse (guaranteed for ten miles) dropped dead before he had gone three!

So, Luther soon began to lose faith in people—and especially religious people, for those who had duped his father had posed as Christians. So, despite the fact his folks were Christians, he struck out to find satisfaction outside Christ. He explains, "I took my eyes off Christ and looked at the hypocrites posing as Christians. Great mistake!"

While attending the University of California at Los Angeles he studied voice under an Italian master and played halfback for the UCLANs (today his physique still suggests football). But when his teacher discovered that he was mixing athletics with music, he drew the line. "To be a great seenger, you must queet football!" the old master exclaimed.

So, Hoobyar, after winning the U. S. Juilliard scholarship in competition with hundreds of other tenors, went to Europe for further study. There a voice instructor prescribed two mugs of German beer before every lesson "if you want to succeed as a dramatic tenor." He took two lessons a day and as a result beer became a habit. This is one of the many habits that disappeared when Christ took over his life.

Later, in the States he sang in many concerts and for the Metropolitan Civic Opera Company and Pacific Opera Company, to name a few. Once while in New York he was called to Hollywood to play a role in a film on Swedish singer Jenny Lind's life, with the late Grace Moore as star. Hoobyar was cast as "Tony," the Italian who conducted Jenny Lind on her tours in Italy. In the picture "Tony" sang four songs and two duets with Grace Moore, all especially composed by Oscar Strauss. In his brief movie career, Hoobyar played a number of other minor roles and now and then was cast in the lead part. He played with such Hollywood names as Clark Gable, the Marx Brothers, Charles Boyer, Rita Hayworth, and Marlene Dietrich. In westerns he was billed as "Steve Ryan."

Naturally, he had many narrow escapes on movie sets as "Steve Ryan," but his most unforgettable experience on the ranges was a real one. He spent two years punching cows and breaking broncos. Once tending a herd of some 2500 cattle, he nestled against his horse White Pacer as both lay relaxing in the grass. This tranquil scene suddenly changed when a jack rabbit frightened the lead bull which started a stampede across the rolling prairie.

Like a flash, Hoobyar was on his horse trying to head off the onrushing herd. But directly in front of the stampede, White Pacer hit a prairie-dog hole and both horse and cowboy sprawled helplessly in the path of the herd. Quickly, Hoobyar scrambled back to the animal and crawled next to his heaving body to try to escape the thundering herd and certain death. White Pacer did not make a move as the frightened cattle rushed over and around him. When the dust cleared and Hoobyar lifted his head, the horse was dead. He had given his life to save his rider!

Luther Hoobyar likes to think of this as an imperfect illustration to give a small idea of what the Lord Jesus Christ did for him—and the rest of the human race. But, like so many people, Hoobyar lived a long time before it finally sank in that Christ had laid down His life for Luther Hoobyar.

The new life that became his upon trusting Christ as personal Saviour that Monday morning after the Easter broadcast thrilled him through and through. When he got up from his knees he awakened his wife, led her to the Lord, then telephoned his aged parents near San Francisco.

The very next Sunday the Hoobyars went down the aisle of a near-by Baptist church and the minister told the congregation of the double miracle. Since then the older boy, Tommy, has been saved and Mary and Luther Hoobyar have led his sister Esther Ann to the Lord.

So, plenty has happened in the life of the Persian tenor since he heard himself sing "The Old Rugged Cross." It is incredible—but true! A man's life changed because he heard himself sing!

...a crumbling stump marks the spot...

16

He Helps
Justice Triumph

On Memorial Day in Chicago in
the middle '40s some 70,000 people—boys and girls, bobby-
soxers, and fathers and mothers—streamed through the gates
of gigantic Soldier Field to attend a long-awaited religious
rally planned by Chicagoland Youth for Christ. Here and
there big Irishmen in blue directed traffic and helped crowds
across streets. To some policemen, the rally was a lot to do
about nothing. Religion, so they figured, was maybe okay
for children and ladies and old people. But not for men,
he-men, that is.

But Chicago police stationed inside the huge lake-side
stadium were in for a surprise. For halfway through the long
program, with newsreel cameras and press photographers
recording the story, a giant of a man wearing a blue uniform
was introduced to the throng. In his brief talk he said
something like this:

"I'm a Christian and want the world to know it. In
my experience I have found that police have to look at the
dark side of life day after day. A policeman's life becomes
perplexing unless he has Christ and enters into some phase

117

of Christian work. Many officers fall into the same sin they see day after day because they have not let Christ take over the reins of their life."

The speaker was Walter F. Anderson, then chief of police of Charlotte, N. C., the largest city of the two Carolinas. He had come to the rally to tell Midwesterners that the Lord Jesus Christ was chief of his life, that in Him he had found peace and satisfaction.

Since the rally Anderson has moved up another niche in the law enforcement business. In April 1946 after considerable prayer he left Charlotte for the state capital, Raleigh, to direct the Bureau of Investigation of the North Carolina Department of Justice. A little FBI, Anderson's State Bureau of Investigation helps track down criminals and put them behind bars anywhere over the 500-mile long Tar Heel state, from the Atlantic Coast to the Great Smoky Mountains in the West. Since his arrival the bureau has grown from ten to nearly thirty employees, including investigators, lab men and clerical help.

Anderson, a strapping 215-pounder, four inches over six feet, has long been one of the outstanding law enforcement men of the South. A lean, lanky State Highway trooper who had never met Anderson six years ago drawled, "He's the most outstanding officer in the state." That was in June 1945 shortly after the Governor asked Anderson to leave Charlotte to head a consolidated State Highway Patrol and Division of Public Safety. He declined the offer, however, feeling that Charlotte still needed a few kinks taken out before he could leave.

I was in Charlotte to interview Anderson the day the Charlotte *News* broke the appointment story under a front-page streamer. But bigger news to Charlotte's chief, I inferred, came from a Charlotte newsman, Dick Young, who phoned that his son Richard, Jr., had been instrumental in launching a Youth for Christ movement on Luzon Island in the Philippines, where he was serving with the armed forces. Anderson had a personal interest because it was all a direct result of a book, *Reaching Youth for Christ*, which he had mailed to the newsman's son.

That June day, as the Governor and the rest of the state awaited Anderson's decision, Charlotte's chief tended to business as usual. Off duty that night, he directed the regular rally of Charlotte Youth for Christ, which he had organized. After the rally, he went home to complete work on a sermon which he delivered next morning in a Methodist church in the Carolina Queen City.

As director of the North Carolina SBI, Anderson has become particularly influential in establishing a sound program of redemption and rehabilitation among prisoners in the state's prison system. He points out that twenty per cent of first offenders return as repeaters and go on to become habitual criminals. Today, as a result of the work of Anderson and other officials, progress is being made. However, the work is still in its infancy and statistics are not available.

To the SBI chief, the most satisfying part of his work comes when he talks about the Lord to those on Death Row in North Carolina's Central Prison at Raleigh. Take the case of James Richard Hall, who was sentenced in Jackson County, N. C., to die for the murder of his sister-in-law, Laura Ellen Taylor, of Dillsboro, N. C. Her body was found under a pile of rocks; evidence revealed she had been strangled and raped. Hall was sentenced to die in the gas chamber in Central Prison on Good Friday, March 22, 1951.

"James Hall was difficult to win for the Lord Jesus Christ because of malice and bitterness in his heart toward his own people because of the fact that they would not come to visit him after his trial," Director Anderson recalls. "We worked with him and prayed for him for seven months before his death."

Long trained to "always get his man," the SBI chief never gave up on Hall and even had part of the state's law enforcement machinery in action before the case was brought to a successful close. Here's how Anderson tells the story:

"On Wednesday before Hall was to die on Friday, I began to pray at home. His situation became such a burden that instead of my returning to the office for work, I went to Central Prison and there talked with him again about his soul's salvation. I was unable to help him, but I did secure permission from him to try to contact his mother.

"On that Wednesday evening at our prayer service in our church, we made this a matter of special prayer and following the service, I called our agent in Waynesville, N. C., some 250 miles away in the western section of the state. The agent, in turn, called Patrolman H. T. Ferguson of the North Carolina Highway Patrol, stationed at Sylva, and Patrolman Ferguson drove into the mountains to the home of Mrs. Hall. He got the mother out of her sick bed and brought her in the patrol car to Sylva where I was privileged to speak to her over the telephone about her son.

"Mrs. Hall stated that she had tried to get her sons and James' wife to visit with him but to no avail. She explained that she had been sick in bed and unable to come. She wanted me to tell James that she still loved him and wanted him to accept Jesus Christ as his Saviour and meet her in heaven. She also told me that she had made arrangements with the local undertaker to come and get his body and return it home for burial.

"With this message from his mother, I went to Central Prison on Thursday morning and talked with James Hall again, giving him the information that I had talked with his mother and that she still loved him and wanted him to receive Jesus Christ as his Saviour and meet her in heaven. James then turned to me and asked me if that was all that his mother said. I did not know how to respond, but felt

120

that I should be frank with him and tell him that she had said also that she had made arrangements with the local undertaker to come and get his body and return it home for burial. The fact that his mother had made this arrangement was evidence to James that she truly loved him and this was the first time he had shown any evidence of real concern about his own soul and salvation. After reading Scripture to him and dealing with him as best I knew how, I then asked him if he had a favorite hymn and he replied that his favorite hymn was 'Amazing Grace, how sweet the sound that saved a wretch like me, I once was lost but now am found, was blind but now I see.'

"I told him that I could do little more for him other than have prayer with him before going. I told him I didn't want to force this on him, but knew of nothing else I could personally do except to pray for him and if he would permit me, I would like to kneel there in front of his cell and have him kneel with me for prayer. He did not answer me for several moments, but then stuck his hands through the cell and warmly grasped my hand and knelt down beside his bunk. I asked the other men on Death Row to sing 'Amazing Grace.' While they were singing, I told James to pray, 'Lord, be merciful unto me and save me for Jesus' sake,' that this was the only prayer I knew he could pray.

"While the men were singing this old hymn, I could hear James Hall praying this simple prayer. Following the singing of the hymn, I prayed for a few minutes and shortly I heard James exclaim, 'It's done!' However, I continued to pray and he continued to speak louder, 'It's done!' And finally he arose from his knees and sat upon his bunk and when I closed the prayer, I asked him, 'What's done, James?'

"He answered, 'Jesus has saved me from sin.'

"Truly this was a great hour and experience in my life because this soul would have gone into eternity on the following morning and now he has been saved for all eternity.

On his face was a radiance and brilliance that I have not witnessed in other conversions. The first thing he wanted me to tell his people was the fact that he no longer resented their failure to visit with him and he had forgiven them. He was asking their forgiveness because of the crime he had committed and the shame he had brought to each of them. He also requested that I tell his mother that he would like to have 'Amazing Grace' sung at the funeral.

"Surely," Director Anderson says, "it is 'amazing grace' that reaches down and saves the vilest of sinners and reaches up and saves the highest respected sinners."

Anderson, now 48, had a personal encounter with the Lord Jesus Christ at the age of thirteen. With a smile revealing a glittering gold tooth, he today relates that it was under an old oak tree during a revival at a Methodist camp ground near Winston-Salem, N. C., that he received salvation through the blood of Christ. Nothing but the crumbling stump of the old oak remains, but it's one of the big SBI chief's favorite spots for quiet meditation with his Lord. He visits there frequently.

Walter Anderson started his career as a policeman in Winston-Salem on his twenty-second birthday anniversary, October 8, 1925, and ten years later was the city's chief of police. He went to Charlotte as chief in 1942. Anderson believes the Lord has protected him from death in several instances. Once a bandit managed to take his pistol in a scuffle and proceeded to empty it at him. However, Anderson fell to the ground and all six slugs passed over and around his body without harm. The North Carolina SBI chief carries a four-inch scar on his left wrist, the result of a wound suffered when an enraged lawyer slashed at him with a knife. The blade narrowly missed ripping into a vital artery. Concerning these brushes with death, Anderson says each has somehow drawn him closer to God.

122

In Charlotte rescue missions Anderson tried to help clean up the Queen City's Skid Row by offering the only lasting remedy for human ills—salvation through Christ. One man's name would have been on a police report had not the Lord reached him through the chief. It happened on Sunday afternoon when Anderson talked to a shabbily dressed man who showed the signs of heavy drinking. The man turned himself over to Christ, lock, stock and barrel. The complete story came out years later, however, when Anderson met the man on the street. Now handsomely dressed, a successful businessman, he introduced himself. Anderson did not remember him until he told his story:

The night he slipped into the rescue mission and found Christ, he had been contemplating suicide. He had left his wife and children, turned to drink and finally despaired of life. He had dropped by the mission on his way to his hotel room, a bottle of poison in his pocket.

So, Walter Anderson's life is packed with thrills around the clock. If he is not helping bring a criminal to the courts of justice, he is tracking down a soul for the Lord. There is adventure in both, but he gets far more satisfaction in seeing a life transformed by the Lord Jesus Christ. After all, snapping handcuffs on a man does not affect the man inwardly. But when the Lord Jesus truly snaps the fetters of sin, handcuffs are never necessary.

As this book was about to be published, Walter F. Anderson left the N. C. Bureau of Investigation to become Director of Prisons for the State of North Carolina. He immediately put into effect a revolutionary rehabilitation program in the state's five main prisons and 85 prison camps, which house close to 10,000 prisoners. He has 1,300 employees under him.

...like Dad...

17

The Man Who
Heads General Shoe

Back in 1919 a man named James
Franklin Jarman faced a problem. Although a partner in a
thriving business, he somehow wanted to get out of it and
start all over, in a brand new field making shoes. What
should he do? He was fifty-five and starting over would
not be easy.

Finally, realizing that the decision could not wait, Jarman
left his office in Nashville, Tenn., and engaged a hotel room
in the little country town of Franklin, 19 miles away. Here,
with Bible in hand, he talked for many hours with the only
One who could tell him for certain the right road to take.

Bespectacled, mustached Jarman told God everything:
Prospects in his present business were good, but he was not
really happy. What he wanted was a business based on
Christian principles, a business in which his partner would
be the Lord Himself. But was a new business possible . . .
wouldn't it be too hard . . . especially at the age of fifty-five
when many men are thinking of retirement?

That day in the hotel room in Franklin, Tenn., James
Franklin Jarman got word from God that he should take the

hard way. So, believing that God would see him through, he started a new business from scratch. Things did not really get rolling until 1924, when on August 5, he got his first retail-dealer order for a small shipment of Jarman shoes. In August 1949, twenty-five years later, 25,419 pins were required to spot the dealers who now sell shoes produced by Jarman's organization.

Today, with more than 10,000 employees, it is known as the General Shoe Corporation, fourth largest shoe manufacturing business in the world and sells shoes around the globe. The more than 16 million shoes produced last year in the organization's twenty-five plants grossed more than $105 million and included shoes for the whole family: for example, Jarman and Fortune for men, Fortunet and Valentine shoes for women, Friendly 'teens for girls, and Acrobat and Storybook for children. They were sold in big and little stores, in the corporation's 260 stores, and "name stores" from coast to coast, including such firms as Geuting's in Philadelphia, The Fair in Chicago, Rich's in Atlanta, Thurston's in Wichita, and Sommer and Kaufman in San Franciso.

James Franklin Jarman has gone from the scene now, but in the driver's seat today is his son, Maxey Jarman, a real chip off the old block. Besides being a business genius like his dad, today's head of the General Shoe Corporation is like his dad in another respect: he, too, is a born-again Christian and looks to God for wisdom in making all decisions.

Chairman of the corporation since 1947 and president for fifteen years before that, Maxey Jarman, whose headquarters are in Nashville, stands firm on issues involving Christian principles. In stockholders' and staff meetings his reports are interspersed with phrases and remarks that bear out his convictions. Not long ago he told thousands of radio listeners, "I believe that Christ should be evident in every phase of my life; so certainly that means in my business. The people

126

with whom we are associated in business are watching us. We want to make sure that they see Christ."

An incident which occurred during the war years in England helps illustrate this. Jarman was in England as chairman of a commission of five men appointed by Uncle Sam to coordinate the requirements of footwear, leather and hides for the two nations during the war. The commission spent about two months making a close study of England's shoe industry. From time to time they attended formal dinners and according to English custom, everyone drank a toast to the King.

Everyone but Maxey Jarman, that is.

His associates were a little embarrassed for him because he either did not drink the toast at all or else drank it in water. Later, however, he met some Englishmen who held similar views, and learned that regulations had been issued by the British Army suggesting water for anyone who did not wish to drink a toast in wine. Jarman's associates finally got around to the point of ribbing him about it, saying surely he must have some bad habits, and that anybody who did not drink, smoke or swear must either lie or steal or something else. But they all seemingly respected his feelings.

Maxey Jarman is not faultless, nor is he a self-righteous, holier-than-thou type of fellow. Lots of people decline cocktails and other intoxicating drinks, he points out. But, like all born-again saints of God, Maxey Jarman stands perfect before God because of his acceptance of Christ as his personal Saviour. In himself he is not perfect, but in Christ he is (I John 1:7).

Jarman, who was born May 10, 1904, made sure of his relationship with God when he was a boy of eleven. Both his father and mother were very active Christians and had daily devotions in their home. So, at eleven, Maxey became conscious of sin, and one time when he was alone he asked Christ to cleanse his heart. That evening he told his mother and father what had happened, and joined the church the following Sunday.

Today one of his close associates describes Chairman Jarman as "a good Christian man." He does not act like a person who feels that he is so much better than his fellow employees, as some in his position might feel. The man Jarman himself stands 5′ 11″, weighs 170, and has reddish gold hair. He has a serious but youthful appearance, dresses meticulously but not extremely, and looks like the busy man that he is. One secret of his success is that he is always ready and willing to try something new. One of his expressions is that "just because we've always done it this way is no reason we have to keep on."

Oddly enough, Jarman began with the organization by showing that he was not afraid to try something new. He was an electrical engineering student at Massachusetts Institute of Technology when his father launched the shoe business. He quit after three years to start in the new business with his father. Jarman began work on a holiday—July 4, 1924—and took home $10 a week to start. His work was varied, running from uncrating machinery and receiving raw materials to acting as secretary of the company, which called for typing letters and other clerical duties. This way he learned something about most phases of the business.

Jarman could be extremely wealthy today if he wanted to be. Naturally, he is well "heeled" but there could have been more. He was slated to receive a great part of his father's large estate, but instead suggested that it be used to set up a foundation, and income from which would be devoted to religious and charitable purposes. Today "The Jarman Foundation" distributes funds to foreign missions, Bible institutes, orphanages, Bible-distributing groups, and many other organizations which are true to fundamental doctrines of the Bible. In the past fourteen years more than a million

128

dollars have been distributed. The Foundation owns about ten per cent of the common stock of the General Shoe Corporation, thanks to the chairman whose gifts have made this possible. This assures the Foundation of additional funds for distribution.

Away from the office Maxey Jarman continues as an influence for Christ. At home, he and his wife have passed on to Franklin, Anne and Gene, their teen-age children, the importance of the daily walk with Christ. They have seen the value Dad places on Bible reading, for they know he reads four chapters a day and that for the last ten years he has read the Bible through each year. Whether it is ping-pong, croquet or taking a brisk morning walk followed by devotions, the family life is Christ-centered.

The family attends a Baptist church in Nashville where Jarman teaches a men's Bible class with an enrollment of 200. Besides teaching, he also is a deacon and serves on various and sundry boards and committees of Christian organizations.

Despite all his activity, Jarman is quiet and reserved. One business associate says he "seems to be slightly self-conscious, could have been bashful." Yet more than once Jarman, whose name flashes above shoe stores from coast to coast, has stepped out from his pew in Sunday evening evangelistic services to speak to someone about his soul. He did that one night recently and one look at his face would have told you that the shoe business was simply a means of making a living. This is natural when Christ gets hold of a man and makes a saint of him.

...China came to him...

18

The Champ Today

T HE WEEK THE KOREAN war broke in 1950, a young man just back from the Far East arrived in Chicago with a timely and challenging story of revival that had swept southern Korea as Red tanks assembled to the north. *Christian Life* Magazine held its presses for the story and called it one of the most important ever printed in the magazine.

The author was one Robert Finley, 1944 national intercollegiate middleweight boxing champion, whose story appeared in *Power* in early 1945. The 1945 article had ended with Finley commenting:

"God hasn't shown me all the details yet [concerning my future]. But one thing is sure: He has called me into full-time service for Him."

After six years, what? I cornered Bob Finley for the answer.

Among other things, I learned that blond, boyish looking Finley, today 185 pounds of man, has traveled more than 500,000 miles with the gospel since hanging up his boxing gloves. War, bloodshed and political strife have dogged his path, but everywhere he has won souls. In Greece he preached during the most tense days of the civil war; in India he won souls and barely escaped a Hindu-Moslem riot; and he preached in Canton the day the new Chinese government opened in early 1949. Another month and he would have been caught in the midst of the Korean war.

Before describing his globe-trotting experiences, Finley reviewed his amazing boxing career. Undefeated throughout his college career at the University of Virginia, he fought his way to the intercollegiate finals at Penn State in 1944. In the final match, he showed up with a bum arm and consequently held little hope of victory. However, despite the handicap, he pounded out a decision over a West Point cadet, to cop the middleweight crown.

Oddly enough, this was not Finley's greatest thrill in boxing. In a team meet at the University of Wisconsin, he entered the ring as underdog in a bout with Chuck Kidd, undefeated Wisconsin KO artist. Unbeaten himself and the Cavaliers' last hope in a losing cause, Bob got these instructions from Coach Truman Southall:

"The best you can hope to do is to defend yourself; so go in there and keep out of the way of that left! It's dynamite!"

Early in the first round Finley boxed cautiously and had little trouble. Then at the half-way mark Kidd ripped a left hook through Bob's defense. The crowd winced at the sickening thud. But Finley did not go down! Like an automaton, he lasted out the round, weaving and bobbing as goggle-eyed fans looked on, amazed. For, although his opponent apparently did not realize it, Finley was *out* on his feet!

The next two rounds were a different story. The Virginia battler recovered to give Kidd a boxing lesson that he probably will never forget. For when Finley was announced

132

as the winner, 15,000 fans, mostly Badger rooters, cheered their approval. Kidd had met defeat for the first time.

However, something had happened before the boxing meet that gave Finley an even greater thrill. In the dressing room the Badger's featherweight boxer asked Bob about things of the Lord and soon yielded to the Saviour. So, later, after the featherweight lost his match, Bob consoled him with: "All things work together for the good . . ." (Romans 8:28, a promise to Christians).

Now and then Finley runs into someone who wonders how he dared to mix boxing and Christianity. "College boxing," he believes, "is decidedly different from professional boxing—it's clean and not nearly as dangerous as it appears. As far as I know it has left no one with permanent injuries. In my books, football and basketball are tougher sports. If a college boxer conditions his body properly, he can absorb plenty without it damaging him physically."

But in any case, boxing is in the past with Bob Finley. *Today* is his great concern now. And whereas before his conversion his ambition was to make a million dollars, today he wants to win a million souls to Jesus Christ. And he is off to a good start:

In early 1950 Finley preached to more than 75,000 in Taegu, Korea, and saw some 2,000 persons take Christ as Saviour. With him preaching the gospel was Missionary-Evangelist Bob Pierce and Gil Dodds, the "Flying Parson" of track fame. Among the huge throng was every public-school student in Taegu, a miracle in itself since only two years before 75 per cent of the students were rabid Communists. Some of these were among converts.

One Taegu convert worked for a newspaper. Next day following the rally he gave his personal testimony in the paper, confessing to having stolen funds from the newspaper. He announced that he wanted to take cuts in his salary to pay back what he had stolen.

Revival had already broken out when Finley arrived in Korea in April. And in city after city he saw men and women fall on their faces in tears of repentance, asking God to have mercy on their guilty souls.

In Seoul a young Communist was transformed by God. "He received faith for fear, love for cruelty, and beauty for ashes," Finley says. "Then he stood up before 10,000 people and gave a public confession of a murder he had committed a few days before."

Perhaps you wonder when Bob got this desire to win souls. It seems it came soon after he finished high school. Born May 2, 1922, into a poverty-stricken farm home near Charlottesville, Va., Bob grew tired of lonely farm life, and ran away to Miami, Fla., after high-school graduation in 1939. And, oddly enough, among his few personal effects was his Bible, although he was not a real Christian. However, he feared dying and liked to read about "eternal life" in the Bible. Fear of death had been with him since childhood, it seems. Once a school chum died suddenly from spinal meningitis, and Bob was particularly struck by the mention of eternal life at the funeral.

In Miami, Bob, reading his Bible regularly, found himself torn between pleasure and eternal life, and after six months eternal life began to win out as the superficiality of the resort center made him turn to a church for fellowship. At Shenandoah Presbyterian Church, pastored by Dr. Dan Iverson, Bob heard the simple gospel story of how he could actually receive eternal life through the Prince of Life, Jesus Christ. He does not know just when, but during those days, perhaps in a Bible class, Bob Finley was born again.

September 1941 found him at the University of Virginia. Living in Randall Hall, Bob started a prayer meeting. Room 37 became known as the preacher's room, and if a fellow needed help this was where he came. Late one night, John Hankins, a serious-minded Southerner, stalked into the room and drawled: "You fellows say you've had a definite experience with Jesus Christ. You've got something I want. I want to be saved." Now opportunities do not usually come like this, so naturally Bob had little difficulty in pointing him to Christ. When Hankins left he was beaming radiantly and carried a New Testament. Bob noticed him next day reading it in the dining hall and between classes as he strolled across the campus. Today, John Hankins is completing his internship at University Hospital, Baltimore. He plans to be a medical missionary.

In 1946-47 Bob did graduate work at the University of Chicago and another chapter of his life began. Living at International House with 650 students from 47 countries, he got a missionary vision as he launched a Bible class, which, incidentally, continues to meet.

Shang-jen Kao, from Peiping, at U. of C. studying for social-service work, attended Bob's Bible class and took a liking to him. He ultimately received Christ and today is back in China, not doing mere social work, but preaching the gospel!

Bob Finley himself originally was called to China as a missionary, but present conditions will not permit his going. So, he is doing the next best thing. "We can't go to China, but China has come to us," Bob says. "There are 5,000 Chinese students here in our universities. Like Shang-jen Kao from Peiping, they will be going back to China within the next two or three years. So we expect to concentrate on winning them to Christ before they leave the country."

Thus Bob Finley, the ex-intercollegiate middleweight boxing champ, is far from being washed up. While he is in a far greater battle than a boxing bout, he is fighting a winning game as a blood-washed saint, giving it all he has until he hears the final bell.

...decided to write a book...

19

He Led the
Pearl Harbor Raid

Remember 1941? In January Hitler threatened to torpedo any American ship that dared bring supplies to the English. In Washington, Congress ignored the threat and voted that taxpayers would foot all bills under Lend-Lease, and, pronto! the throttle of industry was pushed wide open. Meanwhile, close observers saw a serious threat developing in the Far East as Japan began misbehaving. But Americans do not scare easily, and by summer boys in training camps were so discontent that they threatened a mass desertion: "Over the hill in October!" Even Congress relaxed and almost ended the draft, finally extending it by just a single vote. So, by December the thing uppermost in the minds of Americans was Christmas. War was far off . . .

But in Japan military planners were preparing a surprise for America and the rest of the world. On paper, they proved with mathematical certainty that American and British naval power was dependent on fixed bases in the Pacific. With such key bases as Pearl Harbor knocked out, Japan could easily get a stranglehold on much of the Far East and enlarge her empire. Only one Japanese, Admiral Isoroku Yamamoto, showed signs of pessimism: "We would have to march into Washington and sign the treaty in the White House." However, hot-headed army leaders were in the driver's seat and told the admiral to hurry on with the attack.

And so it was on December 7, with the admiral sending his transports south as a decoy to deceive nodding military men in Hawaii, that six aircraft carriers got set for the ambush. At 6 A.M., with the exultant shout of "banzai!" from Japanese officers and crewmen, the carriers launched their first wave of 183 planes to attack Pearl Harbor, 275 miles away. In the first plane 38-year-old Captain Mitsuo Fuchida, the squadron's chief commander, soon ascertained that the main force of the American Pacific Fleet was anchored in Pearl Harbor. His pulse quickened as he saw the sight: eight powerful unsuspecting warships! Behind him now were 359 other planes, all loaded with death. Approaching Ford Island's "battleship row" at 7:55 A.M., Mitsuo Fuchida lifted the curtain of warfare by dispatching the cursed order: "Whole squadron, plunge into attack!"

Fuchida himself was first man over the target and the last to leave it. A bomb from his plane sent the battleship *Maryland* to the bottom, amidst swirling pillars of smoke.

Casualty lists later revealed that the attackers sank six battleships, burned up 164 planes and killed more sailors than the Navy lost in World War I—2,008!—plus 218 soldiers, and 109 marines and 68 civilians.

War had dropped from the sky! Thousands in America rushed to enlist; others volunteered to work long hours in factories; President Roosevelt declared that December 7 "will live in infamy."

Meanwhile, Captain Fuchida and his fliers conquered new territory. And Americans ached for a chance to get their gun sights on them. One by one many of these men fell from the skies: six of the sneak-attack commanders and 32 squadron leaders did not survive the bloody months that followed.

138

Captain Fuchida himself escaped this fate but had many brushes with death.

He crashed at sea six times. And shortly before the battle of Midway he underwent an appendectomy on board ship. Though he did not fly, he was in the thick of that battle. A bomb exploded on his ship, breaking both his legs and hurling him into the sea, from which he was rescued and sent back to Japan. Had he not been out of action he would have commanded the Japanese air force at Guadalcanal and might well have met the fate of many of his fellow officers.

But God had other plans for Captain Mitsuo Fuchida. Today, after a personal encounter with the Lord Jesus Christ, the Prince of Life, he has become a powerful instrument for good. Instead of raining death from the skies, he is firing the mighty "gospel gun," as he distributes New Testaments throughout Japan for the Pocket Testament League, an American organization. His amazing testimony has been used of God to point many other Japanese to the Lord Jesus Christ.

Fuchida, born December 3, 1903, on a Japanese farm, found eternal life at the end of a long search. Following the war — and 25 years of navy service — he retired and began farming.

Curiously, as he continued living in closer relation to the earth, his mind gradually turned to wonder about the One who made the earth and the sky and causes plants to grow. Soon he felt ashamed of his former godless idea that man's own power and ability was his only trustworthy resource. Though he had never considered himself an atheist, he had little religious training and adopted the "War Catechism" upon entering the navy.

Finally, with Japan advocating "Peace" as its reconstruction slogan, Fuchido decided to write a book. In *No More Pearl Harbor* he would campaign for the transformation of hatred among mankind to true brotherly love. He believed that so long as mankind remained in opposition to one another within the frame of nationality, the only consequence could be the destruction of civilization.

But who or what could accomplish this Gargantuan task? One day in Tokyo at Shibuya railroad station Mitsuo Fuchida got his answer. He was handed a pamphlet entitled, "I Was a War Prisoner of Japan," by Jacob DeShazer, one of the Doolittle fliers who made the initial raid on Tokyo and later in a Japanese prison found salvation in Christ.

"At first glance my mind was captivated," Fuchida recalls, "and I read the pamphlet through with great enthusiasm. One portion interested me particularly, and that was the confession of Mr. DeShazer that during his imprisonment he one day came to feel a strong desire to read the Bible. He recalled that he had heard about Christianity which could transform human hatred to true brotherly love."

This caused Fuchida to buy a Bible and before he read the first 30 pages his mind was strongly impressed and captivated.

"This is it!" he said to himself. He concluded that the true realization of his *No More Pearl Harbor* would not occur until Christ Himself returned to reign over the earth. So, he determined to help prepare men for the welcoming of Christ at His Second Coming.

But first he himself must become a Christian. But how? Should he join a church? Try to follow Christ's teachings? Live up to the Ten Commandments? Just *how* would he actually become a Christian?

On the back of the tract he had received in the Tokyo railroad station was the name of the Evangelical Alliance Mission. Following this clue, he visited the mission. Veteran missionary Timothy Pietsch and Glenn Wagner, former Illinois football star and Pocket Testament League representative, opened God's Word there. They showed him clearly the steps of true conversion: (1) repentance of sin; (2) turning from sin; (3) acceptance of Jesus Christ as personal

140

Saviour from sin; and (4) obedience to God. Fuchida opened his heart and asked the Son of God to cleanse him and abide within. And believing that God heard his prayer of faith, the man who led the Pearl Harbor raid suddenly became a Christian—*he became a brand new person in Christ!*

Fuchida immediately began a new warfare—this time upon Satan, as he spoke in Pocket Testament League meetings in Japanese communities and helped distribute Pocket Testament League Gospel portions. In his home town, Mise, Nara, Prefecture, Fuchida arranged a gospel meeting that attracted some 2,000 persons. In this town, where Japan's first emperor introduced Shintoism and where Buddhism was supposedly preached for the first time, 200 Japanese professed Christ as Saviour. Today many of these Christians are holding Bible classes in their own villages. One man volunteered to loan a plot of land so that a church could be established!

During the first months following his conversion, Fuchida received more than 200 letters. Some were congratulatory wishes from Christians, others were from Japanese who wanted to know how to become true Christians. A few letters denounced him for his stand, including two from Communists. The Communist writers advised him to be "cautious because no small influence would be brought about" by his testimony. They told him that peace would never be realized through Jesus Christ, but through the ideology of Lenin-Marx. Fuchida, they thought, would do well to show such earnest zeal toward communism as he does toward the Bible.

But Mitsuo Fuchida knows better. Now for the first time in his life, the man who led the Pearl Harbor raid has peace in his heart! And he plans to continue telling the Japanese people how they, too, can find lasting peace!

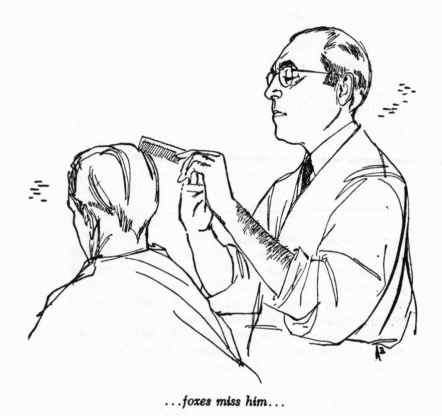

...foxes miss him...

20

37 Years in
a Barber Shop

Wʜᴇɴ ɪᴛ ᴄᴏᴍᴇs to some things Homer Ward can be pretty stubborn. For instance, some time ago he was shaving a customer in his barber shop in Asheville, North Carolina, and at the same time listening to a gospel radio program. The man in the chair moved uneasily, then muttered through thick lather, "Of all the things to listen to on the radio! Cut that stuff off."

Barber Ward did not answer as he applied the razor. Meantime, the radio preacher kept preaching; finally the barber addressed his customer: "No, there's lots of people who need that kind of preaching. So I think we'd better leave the radio as it is."

With that the customer sat up, glared at the barber and reached for his coat. The lather still on his face, he strode angrily out of the shop, banging the screen door behind him. Homer Ward has never seen him since, but he has not worried about losing his trade. "Every time one man has rejected the gospel in my shop," he says, "the Lord has sent me two more customers."

Barber Ward, a husky 195-pounder an inch short of six

feet, by no means makes a practice of driving away trade with the gospel. But the proprietor of popular Crystal Barber Shop, located a stone's throw from Asheville's busy Pack Square shopping district, at the same time does not believe in pulling punches. In all of Ward's thirty-seven years as a barber, this gospel-rejecting customer was the only one to leave mad, foaming at the mouth. Even if the barber shop talk does not swing around to spiritual things, customers can hardly leave without knowing the truth. Over the cash register hangs a blue-and-white sign proclaiming, "Christ died for our sins."

"For eighteen years that sign has caused a lot of men to think. Many are more careful about their language and swearing," Barber Ward says. But from time to time someone slips up. If he finds a tactful way to do it, the barber reproves the foul-mouthed customer. For instance, one afternoon two rangy mountain boys ambled into the shop and began swearing and telling dirty jokes. Quietly, Ward turned from his chair and customer and slipped two little red booklets from a drawer, then stepped over to the offenders. "Here are two little books; read them sometime—lot of good in them." As Ward returned to his job, the boys were staring speechlessly at Gospels of John. Quickly the atmosphere changed. For now the two waiting customers began talking about having praying mothers. Incidentally, they've patronized the Crystal Shop regularly since.

The incident must have reminded Homer Ward of his own past. He himself was born in a mountain home, near Sylva, North Carolina, within sight of the Great Smokies. He had a praying mother and dad, Lucinda and Arch Ward. But in his late teens, he began sowing the proverbial wild oats. Just the same, he believes, God's hand was on him even then. Twice he had narrow escapes. The first time a drunken chum tried to raise trouble with him on a train. Later, off the train, he cursed Ward, who, enraged, landed a

144

nasty blow on his jaw. Suddenly the other youth drew a pistol and fired widly. Fortunately a passer-by halted the pistol wielder before any damage resulted.

Barber Ward's next affray found Ward himself cast in the role of the gun-totin' mountain boy. About twenty-five then, he decided to get even with a man who had shot his brother, Berry. With moonshine liquor under his belt and a pistol on his hip, Ward went to a county election to smoke out the scoundrel. One word brought on another and finally a street fight broke out. Ward, like the chum in the other incident, went after his pistol. But again on-lookers suddenly stepped in and halted the affray. Today, Ward thanks the Lord for keeping the action from going further in both instances.

Ward began barbering in 1914 in Sylva but his shop was not run on today's sound basis. Instead, for the first ten years he was unsaved and his shop smelled of moonshine as well as hair tonic. Then in 1924, after he had married and moved to Asheville, he ran across one of his old drinking friends. Now, though, the friend had changed, was saved and preaching the gospel. He knew that Ward was depending on his own goodness to save him; so he patiently explained that human goodness is never enough, but faith in Christ's sacrifice at Calvary is necessary to bring true salvation. Thus at a meeting in a Baptist church, Ward, with his wife, Viola, was saved "in the old-time way." An elderly lady whom Ward hated went to the mourners' bench with him. And there, somehow, the old grudge left him and love took its place.

But sad to say, business at the shop went on about as usual, though the smell of whiskey disappeared. "I didn't think that Christianity would work in business," Ward admits. "Why, I thought it would never do to bring Christ down to the barber shop." But even so, the fellows at the shop began noticing a change in his life. His well-known temper became subdued and he quit swearing. But conversation about the Lord was reserved for Sundays and revival meetings.

Then a few years later a preacher-barber went to work at the Crystal Shop. Billy Howell, Proprietor Ward noticed, seemed to talk naturally about spiritual things. So the two of them soon had an open Bible there in the shop and during slack periods would discuss the Scriptures together.

But thirteen years ago something happened that really got Homer Ward on the right road for all time. His wife underwent an appendectomy, complications set in and her life hung by a thread. At his wife's bedside, Ward made a covenant: "Raise her up, Lord, and I'll do anything You want me to do."

Homer Ward, unlike a lot of people who make covenants with the Lord, stuck to his promise when his wife regained her health: he started a family altar in his home, went to work at the church, and every day took Christ to the barber shop.

Since that time he's been so busy in the Lord's work that he finally gave up his favorite sport: fox hunting. "Not that there's anything wrong with hunting," Ward points out, "but it was taking too much of the time the Lord wanted." Thus he sold his twelve hounds, which had marked him as one of the mountain area's best-known fox hunters.

Now he has time for work with an evangelistic club as well as an important place in church activities.

Barber Ward gets in plenty of spiritual punches away from the shop as well as at work. Only recently he and a friend, Bert, a coal dealer, called on a retired railroader, an old buddy whom they felt needed a real encounter with Christ. As they knocked, they held their breath, fearing that the old man's hard-boiled daughter would be there. Instead, though, they heard the old railroader call weakly, "Come in."

Earnestly, Homer and Bert talked to the old man about his soul. He believed the Bible, he said, but Christ had never meant anything to him personally. After seeing the plan of salvation clearly, the old man yielded his heart to the Saviour. He died within a month. His hardened daughter, who later said she resented their seeing her father, has never yielded her heart.

Another aged man stands out in Ward's memory. About eighty-five, he lived at the county home, where Ward and other Christian workers held a monthly meeting. The barber began by talking to him about the goodness of the Lord. "The Lord has been good to you. Have you been good enough to serve Him?"

"No," the bedfast old fellow admitted sheepishly.

"Well, isn't it about time you gave the rest of your days to the Lord?"

"I've been thinking about it."

"Well, do you know of a better time than today?"

The old man's face lit up as he admitted, "No I don't." And there he believed and gave a wasted life to the Lord. For many years Ward saw him each month at the county home and got reports that the old man frequently testifies.

So with such experiences as these, Homer Ward has learned that a Christian barber needs to constantly wield something sharper than a razor: the Word of God!

...skipped Sunday School...

I Die at Midnight

by Ernest Gaither, Jr.,
as told to the author

WHEN YOU READ THIS, I'll be dead. Don't be alarmed at hearing from a dead man. For now, as I begin this story, I'm very much alive. It's September 9, 1947—Tuesday. Midnight Thursday I am scheduled to die for murder. Sitting here in my cell in Cook County Jail in Chicago, I've been doing lots of thinking. Some of my thoughts—a warning to criminals—were published in a "note to tough guys" in today's *Chicago Tribune*. This afternoon I read the note on a radio broadcast. But that was really just part of my story.

The real story, I feel, lies in the fact that I don't mind talking about dying. I'm a Negro, just 23 years of age, but I'm ready to go, you see. Why if my number were up this very minute, I'd be ready to meet God. I'm really happy. Just this week I had a dream that I'll carry with me to the chair. I was on my way to heaven. Jesus was with me. But I was taking four steps to His two. He asked me why I was going so fast. I told Him I was eager to get there. Then I was there, surrounded by numerous angels.

Some folks might think that's strange talk from a man who came to jail an atheist. But that's just the way I feel. You'll understand better when I tell you how I met God early one morning.

But first, take a glance at my past. Seven years ago I was a stickup man, head of my own gang of tough guys. There were eight of us. One was Earle Parks, dubbed "Smiley" because he would kill you with a smile on his face. Another was Charles Jones, known as "Pretty Boy" because he was a nice looking guy. The others: Herbert Liggins, known as "Hop-a-long" because he had a bad leg. William Lee was called "Wild Bill" and Charles Hill was known as "Colorado Kid." Clyde Bradford was so dark that we called him "Blue." "The Wheeler" was Percy Bellmar. We nicknamed him that because he was a good driver, my number-one wheeler. All are in prison except for Parks and he died for murder.

They called me "Little Gaither, the Money Waster and Woman Chaser." I tried to act the big shot, always flashing a big roll—sometimes two or three grand.

I started all this when I was just a kid. My folks wanted me to go to Sunday school and church. More than once they gave me a quarter to go with my younger sisters. But I never went. Instead, I'd make them promise not to tell and then I'd go to a movie. I'd stay in the show most of the day and tell my folks that I'd gone to church. They didn't know the difference.

Crime was in me and the movies I saw helped give me ideas. I got some good tips on "how to do it." I remember when I saw the movie, "I Stole a Million," I sat there wishing that I'd been the guy who got the million.

I decided on a boxing career because I thought I was tough and could take care of myself. It would beat working, I figured. I was one of the best fighters in my class for a while. I turned pro in 1938 and fought as a middleweight and ended up in the light-heavy division. Jimmy Bevins was the only man ever to knock me out.

At 18 I was in the Illinois State Training School for Boys, for armed robbery. In October 1941 eight of us made a break but the following month I found myself resentenced to Joliet penitentiary. I had life for a Chicago park murder but got out on parole in June 1946. It looks as if that would have been a lesson to me, but it wasn't.

Within six months after I was out, I was leading another gang. That lasted until last February 9. That night three of us held up Max Baren, 49, in his liquor store on Chicago's West Side. Baren reached for a gun. I yelled at him to put the gun down, but he meant business. I knew it was us or him. So I shot Baren and killed him. We ran out with the money, just $300 which I later gave to the other guys. I went to New York, then to Atlanta, where police nabbed me.

Then weeks later, I stood in a Chicago court.

"Guilty as charged . . ." came the jury verdict.

". . . sentences you to die . . ." the judge said sternly.

And thus I went to Death Row.

Not long after I was placed behind the bars last March 23, a woman of my own race—Mrs. Flora Jones, of Olivet Baptist Church—invited me to attend a prisoners' gospel service. I was playing cards with some other fellows at the time and laughed at her. "Why, I don't even believe there's a God," I boasted, and went on playing cards, the woman still pleading with me. Actually I felt so sinful, that I didn't want to know about God even if He existed. So I ignored her.

Suddenly, something she was saying caught my attention. "If you don't believe in God," she called from outside the bars, "just try this little experiment. Before you go to sleep tonight ask Him to awaken you at any time; then ask Him to forgive you your sins." She had real faith. It got a hold of me.

I didn't go to the service but I remembered the experiment.

"God," I mumbled as I lay on my cot, "wake me up at 2:45 if You're real."

Outside it was wintery. Windows on the inside were frosted. For the first few hours I slept soundly, then my sleep became restless. Finally, I was wide awake. I was warm and sweating, although the cell was cool. All was quiet except for the heavy breathing of several prisoners and the snoring of a man near by. Then I heard footsteps outside my cell. It was a guard, making his regular check. As he was passing, I stopped him. "What time is it?" I asked.

He looked at his pocket watch. "Fifteen to three—"

"That's the same as 2:45, ain't it?" I asked, my heart taking a sudden leap.

The guard grunted and passed on. He didn't see me climb from my cot and sink to my knees. I don't remember just what I told God but I asked Him to be merciful to me, an evil murderer and sinner. He saved me that night I know. I've believed on His Son Jesus ever since.

I'd promised a whipping to another prisoner the next day. That morning I went to him. He backed off. "I don't want to fight you; you used to be a boxer," he said.

"I don't want to fight," I said. "I just came to see you." Several prisoners had gathered for a fight and were disappointed.

But God had saved me from my sins—why should I want to fight? Later it was whispered around that I was putting on an act, trying to get out of going to the chair.

My case did later come up before the Illinois Supreme Court, but they upheld the death sentence. Sure, that jolted me some, but I haven't lost faith in God. I know He will go with me. So, you see, I'm really not afraid.

Before I die I want to leave one last message for other young people:

Start serving the Lord while you're young. Grow up this way and it'll keep you straight. Once crime gets a hold of you, it's hard to stop. Just like the habits of smoking and drinking, if they once get a hold of you, you can't quit.

Yes, I'll be dead when you read this, but please take my advice: ". . . the wages of sin is death; but the gift of God is eternal life through Jesus Christ our Lord" (Rom. 6:23). I found out it's true.

September 10, 1947
Cook County Jail

Today, Warden Frank Sain told me that Governor Green had granted me a stay of execution until October 24.

October 22, 1947
Cook County Jail

Today, I posed for the picture you see with this story. I'm still happy and unafraid. I die at midnight tomorrow.

(*Pete Tanis, then a prison-gate missionary from Chicago's Pacific Garden Mission, takes up the story here and describes Ernest Gaither's last hours on earth.*)

I was admitted to Ernest's cell about an hour before midnight. The atmosphere seemed charged and guards who stood about his cell kept talking to keep his mind off the midnight journey. But things they said were strained and meaningless, like the things you say when you don't know what to say.

As I entered, Ernest smiled and greeted me. A Negro chaplain was reading with him from the Bible. He gave me the Book and asked me to read. I selected the first chapter of Philippians. Ernest leaned forward intently as I read:

153

"For to me to live is Christ, and to die is gain . . . For I am in a straight betwixt two, having a desire to depart, and to be with Christ; which is far better . . ."

This seemed to be a favorite with him, along with the Twenty-third Psalm. He got a lot of comfort from Psalm 23:4: "Yea, though I walk through the valley of the shadow of death, I will fear no evil: for thou art with me; thy rod and thy staff they comfort me." He quoted this from memory, as the clock ticked away the last hour of his life. Outside, the guards listened quietly, some wet eyed.

About 11:30 we had a song service. Ernest said he'd like to sing "When the Roll is Called Up Yonder" and soon the corridors rang with music as a Negro's high tenor voice rang out above the off-key voices of the guards.

As the last strains of another song, "Just a Little Talk with Jesus," was dying away, guards came with clippers to give a haircut to the man with the tenor voice.

Just before midnight Ernest prayed. "God," he began softly, "when I first came here, I hated these guards. But now, God, I love 'em—O God, I love everybody." Then he prayed for people he'd made suffer, for his mother, that the Lord would bless her. "And, Lord," he concluded, "I'm not going to die of electrocution—I'm just going to sit in the chair and go to sleep . . ."

A moment later a black hood was slipped over his head and he began the last mile. At each side were guards, both noticeably nervous. Ernest sensed it: "What are you fellows shaking for? I'm not afraid."

Now 75 witnesses looked on as unsteady hands strapped the hooded figure into the big black chair, accentuated against a stainless steel floor. Then for two minutes—hours, it seemed—an attendant worked feverishly on a defective electrode.

154

Finally, at 12:03 A.M., the first of three electrical shocks flashed through his body.

By 12:15 five doctors had paraded up, and one by one, confirmed the death.

But I knew that the real Ernest Gaither still lived—only his body was dead. As I left the jail, I thought of the verse he liked so well: "For to me to live is Christ, but to die is gain."

"...*packed and ready*..."

22

Case of the
Singing Pilot

On A SPRING EVENING in 1943
Army Air Force men in the control tower at the air base in
Chico, Calif., passed the time with usual small talk. Business
was slow, the sky was clear and the stars were coming out.
Only occasionally did they send a plane into the air or bring
a pilot in for a safe landing.

Meanwhile, in Bellingham, Wash., hundreds of miles to
the north, a middle-aged woman sat at a piano playing favorite
hymns. On the piano was the picture of her son, Dick, an
AAF lieutenant, and she played some of the hymns he had
especially liked to sing with her before going away. For a
moment she quit playing and, bowing her head, asked God
to "give Dick an opportunity to use his voice even at that
moment to His glory and to the salvation of precious souls."

Back at the control tower, as she prayed, operators
suddenly became quiet. Over the amplifier a happy song
was being sung with feeling by a male voice. Had some
pilot gone off his nut? They looked at each other and
listened. A smile crept over their faces. There was only

157

one flier at the base with a trained voice like that—Lt. Dick Knautz. They listened to the end:

"Got any rivers you think are uncrossable?
Got any mountains you can't tunnel through?
God specializes in things tho't impossible;
He does the things others cannot do."*

As the pilot ended his song, the officer in charge of the tower blurted good-naturedly into the mike: "Knautz, if you want to start a revival, come down to earth!"

In his plane, Lt. Knautz glanced at his transmitter and his heart skipped a beat and, unknown to him, his song had been heard not only in the control tower but by every pilot in the starry skies over Chico. He had accidentally left his transmitter open. Quickly explaining his error, he announced that he would accept the officer's challenge, that he *would* come down and "start a revival."

Known by his buddies at the air base as a solid, dependable fellow who lived close to God, Lt. Knautz brought his plane in and made his way to the control room. He prepared himself for some good-natured ribbing for his unplanned broadcast.

However, the tower men seemingly were sincere in their invitation, because each listened intently as the pilot-singer explained Scripture from his Testament, clearly showing that God has provided Christ as man's only hope for salvation; that God and *only* God can provide salvation and that man is hopelessly lost without receiving Christ as personal Saviour. This, he explained, was what he was singing about: ". . . He does things others cannot do."

Several men wanted prayer and when Lt. Knautz left the tower that night no less than four men had confessed their sins and turned to Christ for salvation.

The little chorus Dick Knautz sang that evening over Chico, Calif., had meant a lot to him over the years. He

* Copyright 1945, Youth for Christ Hymnal, Alfred B. Smith, owner. Used by permission.

had sung it many times while a student at Bob Jones College, then located in Cleveland, Tenn. Originally the words of the rhyme were not sacred, but were used by construction workers when the Panama Canal was being dug. Oscar C. Eliason, of Cook, Minn., later changed it slightly to make it a Christian chorus.

Today the picture of Lt. Knautz is still on the piano where he and his mother often sang the little song, along with gospel songs, and majestic old hymns. Dick and his mother were close, and she will always remember that prayer that God answered in leading Dick to sing the chorus at just the right time when the control tower operator would hear it.

Dick wrote his parents about the incident, then later another letter followed. It came on May 7, 1943, and the Knautzes nodded as they read the familiar scripture: "And we know that all things work together for good to them that love God, to them who are called according to his purpose" (Rom. 8:28).

In the letter he also wrote: "Lois [Dick's wife] and I are all packed and ready to go when I receive my transfer orders—which reminds me of how quickly, or rather, how we as Christians should be ready to go at a moment's notice . . ."

Unknown to the Knautz family in Bellingham, Dick that morning volunteered on his day off to relieve a friend and fly with a student on a check ride. But as they flew a wing crumpled and the plane plunged to earth . . . and Dick heard the Signal from another Control Tower and came in for a safe landing to be with his Saviour.

Next day he would have been 23 and would have received his promotion to captain. But there's no doubt: Dick Knautz's promotion was infinitely greater. Like he wrote Mom and Dad, it pays to "be ready to go at a moment's notice."